"Over the course of the book, [Poole's] naïve confidence is tested by a series of loony relatives, sadistic neighbors, and unexpectedly poignant tragedies, and this slightly more re- latable but equally witty David Sedaris type realizes that he is not, in fact, God or even Endora, and that he needs to stop believing in magic and start believing in something he never considered: himself."　　　　　—*Modern Tonic*

"Unflinching [and] infused with love."
　　　　　　　　　　　　　　　　—*St. Louis Post-Dispatch*

"Eric Poole's got the right mixture of being unforgivably witty, embarrassingly dorky, and endearing without being overly sentimental, and he clearly isn't afraid of stripping himself emotionally naked for the sake of a bold laugh."
　　　　　　　　　　　　　　—Laurie Notaro, author of
　　　　　　　　　　　　The Idiot Girls' Action-Adventure Club

"Poole grew up in the Midwest in a family, and among an as- sortment of characters, destined to end up in a coming-of-age memoir. Some of the more entertaining stories include the chaos of his parents' fighting in 1969; the author's befriend- ing of the sarcastic, armless Stacy; his magical obsessions with *Bewitched*, which included an unhealthy attachment to Endora; and his failed exorcism of another boy in Bible School. From his early childhood, when he escaped into his family's basement to chant magical charms to ward off alienation and chaos, through his teenage years, when the normal teenager panic was amplified by the added bewil- derment of his awakening homosexuality, Poole shares an intimate, self-effacing chronicle of a unique young boy and the forces that molded him into the grounded, articulate, charming oddball he is today."　　　　　—*Kirkus Reviews*

continued . . .

"Engagingly large-hearted. The author's humor is largely character-driven, focusing on his long-suffering father, his older sister, and his cleanliness-obsessed mother, who would be more than a match for Mr. Clean. Poole has his own obsession: Endora from *Bewitched*. Whenever things get tough, he dons a white chenille bedspread and becomes the Endora of St. Louis, imagining magical solutions to his many problems—bullies, his parents' arguments, an enforced camping trip with mannish Aunt Jinny, and his growing awareness of his homosexuality—with mixed success. Somewhere along the line, Endora is replaced by God, who doesn't seem much more reliable, though Poole does become a demon trumpet player, which may—by the time he's in high school—open the door to peer acceptance. Readers will be rooting for him."   —*Booklist*

"It made me jump up and down and holler 'Yummy!' like my grandmother Mary Lucille's red velvet cake."
          —Leslie Jordan, author of *My Trip Down the Pink Carpet*,
                    and costar of *Boston Legal* and *Will & Grace*

"Fragrant as it is of Love's Baby Soft perfume and hormones, Poole's memoir of growing up gay and Baptist in the seventies would be worth reading if it were just gut-splittingly funny. But *Wand* is also a deeply moving account of a boy's attempt to control his world with his own brand of magic. That world includes his sometimes terrifying family [and] an armless best friend. . . . It's Poole's mother, though, who is the standout character. Annihilating and loving by turns, she makes Sophie Portnoy look like June Cleaver, yet Poole finds her humor and humanity."   —*People* (★★★★)

Where's My Wand?

ONE BOY'S MAGICAL TRIUMPH

OVER ALIENATION AND

SHAG CARPETING

Eric Poole

B

BERKLEY BOOKS

New York

THE BERKLEY PUBLISHING GROUP
Published by the Penguin Group
Penguin Group (USA) Inc.
375 Hudson Street, New York, New York 10014, USA
Penguin Group (Canada), 90 Eglinton Avenue East, Suite 700, Toronto, Ontario M4P 2Y3, Canada
(a division of Pearson Penguin Canada Inc.)
Penguin Books Ltd., 80 Strand, London WC2R 0RL, England
Penguin Group Ireland, 25 St. Stephen's Green, Dublin 2, Ireland (a division of Penguin Books Ltd.)
Penguin Group (Australia), 250 Camberwell Road, Camberwell, Victoria 3124, Australia
(a division of Pearson Australia Group Pty. Ltd.)
Penguin Books India Pvt. Ltd., 11 Community Centre, Panchsheel Park, New Delhi—110 017, India
Penguin Group (NZ), 67 Apollo Drive, Rosedale, Auckland 0632, New Zealand
(a division of Pearson New Zealand Ltd.)
Penguin Books (South Africa) (Pty.) Ltd., 24 Sturdee Avenue, Rosebank, Johannesburg 2196, South Africa

Penguin Books Ltd., Registered Offices: 80 Strand, London WC2R 0RL, England

The publisher does not have any control over and does not assume any responsibility for author or third-party
websites or their content.

PRINTING HISTORY
Amy Einhorn Books / G. P. Putnam's Sons hardcover edition / May 2010
Berkley trade paperback edition / June 2011

Berkley trade paperback ISBN: 978-0-425-24101-1

The Library of Congress has cataloged the Amy Einhorn Books / G. P. Putnam's Sons
hardcover edition as follows:

Poole, Eric, date.
Where's my wand? : one boy's magical triumph over alienation and shag carpeting / Eric Poole.
p.   cm.
ISBN 978-0-399-15655-7
1. Poole, Eric, date—Childhood and youth.   2. Saint Louis Region (Mo.)—Biography.   I. Title.
CT275.P6812A3   2010   2009051233
977.8'66043092—dc22

PRINTED IN THE UNITED STATES OF AMERICA

10   9   8   7   6   5   4   3   2   1

*Penguin is committed to publishing works of quality and integrity.
In that spirit, we are proud to offer this book to our readers;
however, the story, the experiences, and the words
are the author's alone.*

To my big-hearted father and sister, for allowing me

to be who I was, even against their better judgment.

And to my beloved and much-mellowed mother,

who has never let me forget that she loves me,

even after reading this book.

If that isn't magic, I don't know what is.

Acknowledgments

Thank you . . .

To my family, who has cheered me on relentlessly, all the while knowing they were being immortalized in ways not always flattering.

To my agent, Rebecca Oliver, who, upon first meeting, flung her arms around me and exclaimed, "I love your book!" And from that moment on, I have loved her back.

To my editor, Amy Einhorn, who gently and patiently and brilliantly forced me to create a better book than I ever could have without her.

To the gifted Terry Wolverton and all my beloved writing buddies at Writers at Work, for their support and inspiration and velvet-knife criticism. Without you, I wouldn't have a book.

And to my partner in life and crime, whose patience and willingness to sacrifice so that I could pursue my dream mean more to me than he'll ever know.

I love you all.

Many names and identifying characteristics have been changed to keep me from getting sued or yelled at in public. A few minor characters are composites to save having to introduce you to the countless number of people who flow in and out of one's life. Some sequences and details of events have been altered so that, like a reality show, you don't have to sit through the parts where characters eat or poop or just stare at each other. What has not been changed even one iota is the journey of self-delusion and self-discovery that I began forty years ago. That part's exactly, embarrassingly, correct.

ONE

The Captain of Chenille

As God is my witness," Mother shouted, "I will not live in this chaos!"

It was a muggy St. Louis summer night in 1969. As our mother screamed at our father behind the closed door of their bedroom—"Did you even get *halfway* through this list?" she hollered, slamming the daily checklist of duties she made for him onto the dresser— Val and I focused on the faint electrical buzzing of the Black & Decker bug zapper hanging over the patio, as it systematically executed unsuspecting mosquitoes.

It was ten P.M. and no one was outside, but our mother kept the zapper running twenty-four hours a day as a silent screw-you to Mother Nature. To offset the cost of this outdoor insect patrol, she set the air-conditioning of our suburban tract home at a toasty eighty-four degrees, so we all slept in small pools of perspiration, secure in the knowledge that those bugs knew who was boss.

I clung to my twelve-year-old sister Valerie, both of us sweating profusely as she climbed into her canopy bed fringed in multicolored hippie beads. She squeezed my hand tightly.

"One day," she whispered, "we'll look back on this and laugh."

"I will not be married to a sloth!" Mother thundered as I quietly reached for Val's dictionary to look up what Dad had just been called.

The bedlam Mother referred to was that created by our father opting to play Kerplunk with Val and me that afternoon, instead of completing item #7, alphabetizing the Christmas decorations stored in the garage, or #13, washing the lightbulbs on the dining room chandelier.

The hippie beads shimmied as Val, my only sibling, settled between the sheets. She was a petite but bossy brunette who spent hours each day ironing her long hair Marcia Brady–straight—in an effort, she told me years later, to distract from the nose that made her appear to be the love child of Karl Malden and Barbra Streisand. As she attempted a smile and turned to switch off the lamp that I had just traded her for the

Diana Ross and the Supremes *Greatest Hits* album (thus unwittingly sealing my sexual identity at the tender age of eight), I began to ritualistically rake the shag carpeting around the bed with an avocado-green plastic carpet rake, vigilantly erasing all signs that anyone had trod upon her floor. The carpet slowly became a pristine meadow of brown, white and gold, a lush, undisturbed wool and nylon Astroturf.

With the well-rehearsed precision of hundreds of nights' practice, I worked my way down the hall, slowly approaching the closet where the rake would be stored upon completion. Fortunately, the closet door—along with all other doors in the house—could be closed without disturbing the integrity of the finished job. Following an apocalyptic moment after the carpet was installed—when our mother discovered that entering a room created the shag version of snow angels—Dad had planed each of the doors, sawing off a full inch of wood at the base, rendering them so high-water that each doorway now appeared to be wearing wooden capri pants.

As I passed the bathroom, Val stuck her head out of her bedroom. "Don't forget to pee!" she whispered, reminding me that I would need to go now or hold it until morning, since Mother tolerated *no* disruptions in the placid waters of this sea of shag once the requisite raking was finished. I had learned not to consume large amounts of liquid before bedtime, ever since the night I had drunk an entire quart of Coke and, in desperation, had tried to pee out the bedroom window screen.

My pursuit of a flawlessly raked floor did not strike me as odd, since perfection was not optional in the Poole family militia; it was compulsory. It was also the means by which I attempted to maintain control over the rapidly shifting ground beneath my feet.

Our family had just moved from Iowa to Missouri for a new and better life. Dad had accepted a job in contract administration with a major aircraft company, and Mother was to become the executive assistant to a corporate chieftain, and together, their new careers were to be the start of a prestigious change of life for the Pooles.

What transpired instead was a series of matinee and evening performances of *Who's Afraid of Virginia Woolf?* sans the Edward Albee script and intermissions, as our parents' relationship seemed to be disintegrating before our eyes, and my sister and I attempted to determine which of us was responsible.

As I worked my way down the hall with the carpet rake, closing in on my parents' bedroom, the level of Mother's voice rose. "How I married someone so completely devoid of competence," she barked, "is an absolute mystery. I had my pick of any man in Kansas City—"

Outside the door, I carefully coaxed each carpet

strand into absolute alignment. There would be no defectors in my Carpet Crusade, no errant soldiers in this battle for perfection.

"The kids can hear you," Dad whispered. "You need to stop this right now."

"Or what?" she hissed. "Don't you dare threaten me."

"I'm not threatening anybody, I'm just saying—"

"You make me sick, you know that?"

The bedroom door flew open. Dad—a slender, six-foot-tall man with a prominent nose and a glossy shock of wavy black hair—grabbed his car keys from the dresser and stomped down the hall.

"Don't leave!" I cried, before even realizing the words had escaped my mouth. I grabbed my father's leg, my hands clutching his ankle.

Mother appeared in the hall wearing a floral print duster and a thick layer of cold cream on her face. She was a petite woman with a stunning figure and a graceful, angular beauty that was, perhaps unsurprisingly, lost on me in this moment.

"Fine. Get out!" she bellowed, as my fingers dug deep into the thin flesh above my father's foot. He moved slowly toward the door, attempting to gently dislodge me as I hung on for dear life beneath a hanging glass swag lamp.

Val had quietly slipped into the family room. She ran to our father. "Take me! You can leave Eric with her," she cried, throwing me to the wolves. "Just take me!"

"Go to your rooms," Mother ordered us. "Both of you!" Neither of us moved, afraid that the consequences of leaving this room would be even worse than disobeying her.

Dad gazed longingly at his offspring for a brief moment, then pushed our hands away and opened the door. Without another word, he was gone.

There was a stunned moment of silence. I lay on the floor, my hands frozen in outstretched plea. Val and I turned to look at our mother, a mix of fear and contempt on our faces, as tears formed in her eyes. She twisted on her heel and swept into the bedroom, slamming the door with such force that the frame threatened to explode.

I stared at my sister, horrified. After a long moment, she moved to pat my back as I began to cry in quick, gulping sobs, unable to catch my breath.

"Well," she declared matter-of-factly, "you're gonna have to rake all over again."

PERHAPS IT WAS events like this that sparked my interest in magic.

Perhaps it was because my new third-grade teacher, a sadist in stilettos named Mrs. Locke, had it in for me. Today, Mrs. Locke would be able to positively channel her aggression into a career as a bounty hunter or an Attica prison guard, but in 1969, her only outlet was a group of unsuspecting third-graders, and one in particular.

Or perhaps it was because I had been given a gift-with-purchase upon arriving at my new elementary school, a sneering bully named Tim who, in concert with Mrs. Locke, conspired to inflict as much emotional damage as was possible at the age of eight, obviously assuming there were prizes involved.

Whatever the cause, I worshipped the TV show *Bewitched*—and, to Mother's irritation, could be found flattening the shag in the family room every Thursday night when it aired. The lovely wife, Samantha, her devoted husband, Darrin, and their spotless suburban home all mirrored my own family's existence, but with a refreshing lack of screaming and crying.

Yet even more alluring was the magic. The notion of being able to snap my fingers, wave my hands or twinkle my nose and magically alter the circumstances of life was intoxicating, akin to learning voodoo or having Jesus owe you one. And the more I watched, the more I became convinced that somewhere within my own being, I must possess similar magical powers.

But whom to model myself after? True, Sam was young and beautiful and smart, but her mother, Endora—there was someone with style. Someone with a flair for the dramatic.

Endora favored caftans, so my search began for an outfit that would allow me to approximate her look. Long, flowing sleeves were especially important, for that theatrical, Endora-style arm flourish as I performed episodes of life-changing magic.

While rifling through a basement closet one day, I stumbled upon an old white chenille bedspread. It was a little threadbare, but at double-bed size, it gave me plenty to work with. The Endora of St. Louis was born.

My becoming Endora was not something I felt my sister Val would embrace. As a rule, she tended not to favor her eight-year-old brother in drag. On the day of my transformation, I waited patiently for Val to leave for her best friend Vicki's house, knowing that she would need to confide in her about our dad's sudden departure the night before.

Vicki McDougal lived up the street, and was quite sexy in a white-trash, I'm-only-twelve-but-I-wear-tube-tops way. I was unclear as to how Val and Vicki passed the time they spent together, but apparently it had something to do with auditioning makeup, since Vicki had a fishing tackle box filled with glitter foundation and blue eye shadow, and Val regularly came home looking like a clown trainee.

Our mother despised the McDougals. "They may not live in a trailer now," she declared, "but those people are one step away from a steering wheel in the living room."

"I'm going to Vicki's," Val announced, adding, "Don't tell Mom, or you'll be the next one thrown out." She slammed the door behind her. I rushed to the window to perform a visual check. Val was half-way up the block, waving a *Tiger Beat* magazine and a bottle of Love's Fresh Lemon perfume at Vicki.

I flew downstairs to the basement, where I had hidden the chenille bedspread behind a mohair recliner. The chair was positioned against the wall, so my parents were unlikely to look behind it, since Mother—despite being a highly motivated neat freak—only lemon-oiled the paneling every few weeks. I pulled out the bedspread, picked off the Acrylon lint from the orange industrial carpeting, and began to carefully drape it over my body, adjusting the sleeves to ensure that they did not flow past my wrists, so as not to interfere with the magic I was sure would be emanating from my hands.

First, I conjured up the image of my new school-teacher, Mrs. Locke. She was a tall, rail-thin woman with high heels and a twelve-inch blond beehive, and she towered over our class in a way that seemed not only menacing but outright dangerous, since her balance frequently appeared to be in peril.

She would lean over her desk, her pinched facial expression giving her the appearance of someone who was constantly sniffing a turd, and snap her fingers. "You! What's your name?" I would scan the room, my head rotating like a police siren, desperately hoping that it was someone else's turn. "Yes, *you*, you idiot, I'm looking right at you." Then, even louder: "DID YOU HEAR ME?"

"My name is Eric," I would reply, smiling angelically in a futile attempt at charm.

She would cross the room to tower before me, Godzilla looming over Tokyo. "Stop rushing through your tests that way, you're not that smart." Mrs. Locke was referring to my penchant for being the first in the class to finish any exam or quiz. By now well aware that I possessed few selling points that those around me seemed to appreciate, I had tried using my intelligence as a method of currying favor, since I usually scored A's. This worked like gangbusters on my art and music teachers, but Mrs. Locke was not the pushover that those creative types were.

"You think you're Albert Einstein," she continued, her voice booming over my head as I looked down, attempting to perform quantum physics by combining my atoms with those of the laminated beige desktop. "Well, we all know what happened to him." Several kids tittered knowingly. Actually, none of us did know, but her ominous tone implied that hurrying through tests would result in some sort of particularly embarrassing or violent demise, like vomiting to death.

Back in the basement, I visualized that moment, contemplating as much of the humiliation as I could bear. Then, with a dramatic wave of my bedspread-laden arms, I disappeared—sailing through the cosmos at lightning speed, passing Venus and Jupiter, waving at angels and demons as I traversed the space/time continuum to return to the beginning of the school year.

I reappeared—now finding myself in a different classroom, with an adoring teacher named Maryann (she insisted that I call her by her first name). She was petite, dark-haired, and had a warm, easy smile. Maryann announced to the students, "Children, I know that I shouldn't have favorites, but . . ." She gazed fondly at me, her eyes misting up. "Eric is just . . . too . . . special."

Maryann kept me after the last bell to give me hugs and show me the test scores of my classmates. We gossiped about the stupid kids, laughing and drinking Yoo-hoo in the forbidden inner sanctum of the teachers' lounge. As Maryann and I walked arm in arm past Mrs. Locke's classroom, chuckling over a private joke, Mrs. Locke, straining to hear, fell off her high heels. She landed on the cold, worn beige tile floor with a loud thud, denting her beehive, giving it the look of a honeycomb frequented by drunken bees.

It was a vastly fulfilling moment.

I thanked Maryann for a wonderful day and bid her farewell, as she handed me a Pixy Stix for the road and wiped a tear from her cheek. Up into the sky I flew, breezing through solar systems as the cosmic dust of passing planets sparkled like glitter.

Suddenly, I began to veer off course, wrenched across the Milky Way by a force not of my own power. Was it a gravitational pull, a black hole, some unnamed, gaping void? I was silently and swiftly sucked into the desolate world of my current schoolyard, where I found myself standing face-to-face with my unbearably attractive bully.

Tim was an athletic, stupid and shockingly handsome boy who was destined to become either a football hero or Prom Queen at the state penitentiary. Although not known for his extraordinary powers of deduction, Tim had discovered the deep, dark secret that I told few people: I was deaf in one ear.

As the new kid in school, with few check marks in the looks and athletic columns, I had concluded that physical impairments would probably not add to my luster. Unfortunately, because I inadvertently ignored Tim whenever he whispered something in my right ear, it became somewhat difficult to camouflage, and between my *I'm sorry, what?*s and Mrs. Locke's repeated *DID YOU HEAR ME?*s, he eventually concluded that I was, in his insightful words, a "one-ear."

Partially hearing the taunts of a bully is difficult enough, but having to ask him to repeat them pretty much assures an impressive level of trauma. I momentarily flashed back to the previous day, when

Tim—who had limited imagination and tended to double up on his material—had whispered, "You can't run, you can't play dodgeball, and you can't hear—you're a triple threat!"

Naturally, all I felt was a rush of air against my neck, so when I turned and, in my most nonthreatening, please-don't-beat-me-up voice, replied, "What did you say?" he repeated it at a volume that would wake Helen Keller. Everyone within two earshots guffawed.

I executed a theatrical Endora-inspired wave, my caftaned sleeves billowing through the air. Tim and I disappeared, swallowed into the earth, screaming through dirt and rock and molten iron, atoms and energy colliding into alternate dimensions. Within seconds or minutes or maybe lifetimes, we reappeared on the playground of our school.

Tim was standing before me. But something was different. He was much more subdued. He slumped a little when he walked. His confidence was shaken. Tim was deaf.

Exhilaration washed over me as I contemplated my sudden advantage. The sheer number and variety of taunts now available was overwhelming: "Hey, no-ears!" or, while flipping him off, "I speak sign language!" or my personal favorite, "You're Beethoven without the talent!" Even though this last one would doubtless go over most of their heads, kids from all corners of the playground would howl with laughter, pointing and sniggering, the raucous jeers slowly building to a, pardon the pun, deafening roar.

But ultimately, I chose silence. Perhaps I was more desperate for friendship than revenge. I picked up a large rubber ball, then backed up across the basement playground. As I prepared to throw it at him, he adopted the official Dodgeball Stance, ready to scamper left or right, and grinned. We began to play.

As the afternoon began to wane, I waved goodbye to Tim and promised to return for a tiebreaker. I waved my arms and began to drift down through the clouds and into the family room of our home, where—in the final moment of my magical conjuring—I now saw Val and me enjoying a wicked game of Chutes and Ladders.

We heard a car pulling into the garage.

"Dad's back!" Val shrieked happily. We threw the door open and ran to greet him at the car. We were not in any way a physically demonstrative family, but in this tender, imaginary moment, as we leaped into his arms, he hugged us tightly, stroking the backs of our heads as he whispered, "Never again. Never again."

Suddenly, I was jolted out of my magical vision by the sight of my sister standing in the basement, reeking of lemon perfume, her eyelids an explosion of electric blue powder.

"Why are you wearing a bedspread?" She eyed me disdainfully.

"How did you get in?" I fumbled defensively. "You left your key here!"

"Vicki has one," Val replied. She surveyed my costume. "So what's with the white cape, Superwoman?"

I yanked the bedspread off, embarrassed. "It's not a cape, it's a . . . okay, it's a cape," I mumbled, realizing this was probably the lesser of two wrong answers. I stood up straight. "I am BibleBoy, Defender of Righteousness."

"Oh, brother," Val replied, rolling her eyes. "You are so *eight*." She thrust her wrist under my nose. "How do I smell?"

That evening, as Val and I performed our dinner ritual of heating Mother's premade frozen casserole, I thought about this near miss, and what would happen if I were ever truly discovered. I would probably be sent to Windermere, the local Christian summer camp, which was Vacation Bible School but with bunk beds and torture (the camp was widely known to be populated by Missouri's top Christian bullies). I vowed to be more careful, lest I end up another casualty of the love of Jesus.

The garage door opener began humming. Mother was home.

Val and I prepared for the theatrics that often accompanied Mother's nightly return. Our afternoon attempts to render the house unlived in, free of all traces of human habitation, usually failed on a scale that could not be measured by existing devices, as her screams of frustration—"GOD IN HEAVENNNN!!"—pierced the evening sky. "WHY, GOD, *WHY* IS THERE WATER IN THIS *SINK*?"

The door opened. Mother stepped into the house, her head bent, a hollow, defeated expression glazing her delicate features. She dropped her purse on the kitchen table, smiled wanly at Val and me, and disappeared into her bedroom.

Silence. Val and I set the table, unable to look at each other. The satisfaction in seeing our mother cowed was overwhelmed by her palpable pain. This was unfamiliar emotional terrain.

Mother reemerged in her "comfy," an ugly print housedress that had been washed several thousand times. We sat down to dinner.

"How was your day?" she quietly asked my sister.

Val, understandably uncomfortable with our mother's sudden vulnerability, threw me under the bus. "I caught Eric wearing a bedspread," she announced.

"It was a cape!" I hollered defensively. "I'm a superhero." Mother turned to me. She smiled somberly and patted my hand.

"You can be anything you want to be."

"He thinks he's BibleBoy or some retarded thing," Val declared.

"That is not *retarded*, young lady," Mother announced sternly. We felt the storm clouds gathering, and began to anticipate an outburst, a flash of anger, a roiling moment of ire that, although difficult, would be familiar.

She turned to me with a fragile smile. "That is something to be proud of," she said softly. "Are you saving the world one soul at a time?"

Before I could answer, the sound of the garage door opening galvanized the room. We turned to our mother as if for direction, unsure what her reaction would be.

Suddenly infused with energy, she jumped up and grabbed a plate and silverware from the cabinets, quickly setting a place for our father. She began to talk quickly, animatedly, making little sense. It didn't matter.

The door opened. We heard our father's footsteps across the family room. He entered the kitchen and took his place at the table, still wearing the same white undershirt, Dacron slacks and moccasins he had left the house in the night before.

"That casserole smells delicious," he declared to Val and me, not looking at our mother. "You can't go wrong with mushroom soup and Funyuns."

"Do Funyuns grow in the ground or on trees?" I asked Dad in a rush of words as he sat down.

"In the ground," he replied, smiling at Val and me without meeting Mother's gaze. "Maybe we'll plant some in the garden," he continued. "It takes a real green thumb to grow 'em with that crispy coating."

Throughout the meal, Mother and Dad never once locked eyes; but it didn't seem to matter. Somehow, a truce was negotiated. Armistice was established. And dinner progressed into a tranquil evening unmarred by outbursts.

And I began to believe that perhaps, with the help of a basement and a bedspread, magic could happen.

TWO

I Saw Mommy Slapping Santa Claus

Dad, Val and I gathered in the rathskeller of our suburban home, nervously awaiting Mother's appearance. It was Christmas Eve, 1969, and although she had not been in a good mood since the mid-sixties, her disposition had grown even more unpleasant since our father had lost his job.

Our rathskeller (the sophisticate's term for a tarted-up basement) was glamorously outfitted with carpet tiles, a Styrofoam drop ceiling and a Ping-Pong table. Because Mother worked as the executive assistant to the president of a large furniture corporation, she got sample sofas on the cheap, so everywhere you turned, there were couches, love seats and chaise longues covered in cotton zebra print or orange corduroy—an eye-catching collection that gave our rathskeller the impressive look of a JCPenney sidewalk sale.

The Poole family rathskeller came into being when, less than a year into the job for which he had moved us to St. Louis, Dad became a casualty of downsizing.

My sister and I learned of this change in employment status the same way we learned about everything important: via a behind-closed-doors discussion between our parents, who were apparently under the impression that the walls of our home approximated a bank vault.

"You moved us down here, and for what?" Mother shrieked. "So I could be the breadwinner?"

"It's not like I planned this," Dad replied defensively. "Who could have seen this coming?"

"Would you like a list?" Mother snapped. "They told you they might be restructuring."

"Pete said my job would be safe."

"Did he also tell you that pigs would be winging their way over the greater St. Louis area?"

Val and I sat on the floor of her bedroom, subconsciously keeping score: Mother, 5, Dad, 0. "Turn it up," I whispered, as Val blasted Bobby Sherman singing "Easy Come, Easy Go" on her Close 'N Play in a futile attempt to drown out the proceedings.

"I'll be getting a month's severance," Dad offered.

"Great," Mother hollered. "That'll give us enough

time to pack before the house goes back to the bank! I'll be sure to leave out the tin cups. We'll need them when we're lying in front of the 7-Eleven, begging for quarters."

Thus began Dad's sojourn in the land of the unemployed. Almost immediately upon finding his days free, Dad realized that the best way to keep busy and out of Mother's gun sights would be to have a project. So he promptly undertook the planning and execution of a rathskeller that became the talk of the Wedgwood Green subdivision. Friends of Dad's dropped by to ooh and aah at the homemade bar (lovingly constructed out of paneling and linoleum) and inquire how we came by so many pieces of unmatched seating. The rathskeller was truly a place for entertaining, and Christmas Eve was bound to be the most entertaining night of all.

THE POOLE HOLIDAY SEASON kicked off each year immediately after Thanksgiving with the trimming of the artificial Christmas tree. It was a silver aluminum affair with a rotating color wheel that, when strategically placed, turned the tree into a fantasy of ever-changing hues. It's blue—no, wait, it's red!

"Can I put the first ornament on?" I yelled to Dad, who was dragging the tree box downstairs, followed by my sister, who refused to lift the other end because she was convinced that at any moment her new train-ing bra—overloaded with mammaries the size of kiwis—might snap.

Dad, Val and I were bundled up like sherpas, since it was freezing in the rathskeller—Mother was always hot, and she kept the house at a temperature that could allow the curing of meats—yet I was practically sweating with anticipation as I rocked impatiently on my heels.

"Are you serious?" Val snorted, flipping open a Merle Norman compact purloined from the Wal-greens by her hot-fingered friend Vicki. "It's still dec-orated from last year." She pursed her lips with all the twelve-year-old seduction she could muster as Dad pulled the tree from the box and set it into its stand. It was indeed loaded down with tinsel and ornaments, not a single branch bare.

"Your mother feels that this is more efficient," he explained to us, "so that we have more time for the things that really matter."

"Like what?" Val replied, snapping the compact shut, evidently satisfied that her lips were properly kissable although, as far as I knew, she had never kissed a boy. "She spends all her time in the laundry room, ironing the bedspreads."

Dad shrugged. "I don't make the rules. I just work here."

Val shot me a "No shit" look as our petite mother,

General Patton in pedal pushers, marched in from the basement laundry room carrying a freshly pressed quilt. "Good thing you work *somewhere*," she replied, as she blew past the tree and up the stairs.

Dad sighed heavily and passed me the electrical plug. I stuck it into the wall socket ceremoniously, and the color wheel lit up. I clapped excitedly as Dad's face turned green, then flaming red. A sign of things to come.

My sister and I had never really believed in the notion of a fat man delivering presents via the chimney, since Mother (a) forbade anyone to use the fireplace, and (b) refused to have all those gifts cluttering up the closets, and instead insisted on wrapping all presents and immediately placing them under the tree upon purchase.

Of course, since she was a busy working woman, she had little time for such mundane tasks as making sure that the wrapping paper covered the entire gift, so one afternoon Val and I rendezvoused under the tree.

"Let's see . . ." Val busily combed through the packages, turning one over to reveal a label easily readable from beneath a two-inch strip of missing paper. "Oh, jeez. Remington hot rollers. For *that* I was nice all year?"

"Look." She pointed as she flipped another box over. "You got Matchbox cars." Not quite the drum set I had hoped for. We looked at each other, deflated. "Guess it's official," Val announced. "We're broke."

Although greedy and selfish like most kids our age, we were ultimately less concerned about the size of the gifts this Christmas than the size of the blowout that would doubtless accompany our celebration. Now that Mother had become the family's breadwinner, her resentment of the slobs she was forced to not only clean up after but also support was palpable. And while she democratically managed to inflict a great deal of this frustration on Val and me, Dad was the jackpot winner. I realized, in that moment, that in order to save us all from a particularly humiliating holiday, Dad—who had never exhibited a high degree of backbone with Mother—would have to take charge.

It had been a few weeks since my last magic spell, which I had performed to excise the murderers Val was certain were waiting for us in the house each day when we arrived home from school. (She would unlock the front door, push it open a few inches and shove me inside, pausing to listen for screams and gunfire.)

Despite having nervously performed that incantation in the basement while Val and her friend Vicki were right upstairs secretly test-driving eyeliner, I had obviously not lost my touch: to date, neither Val nor I had been slain in our suburban home.

My magical abilities were obviously becoming keen, and not a moment too soon, because one December afternoon, in some perverse stab at either reassurance or denial, Dad made an ill-conceived announcement.

"I'm gonna surprise your mother with a couple of unexpected gifts," he confided as we sterilized the kitchen in preparation for Mother's arrival home. "Is that okay with you kids? You know we're not gonna have a big Christmas this year, but your mother works so hard. She deserves something special, don't you think?"

Her cataclysmic mood swings aside, we did have to admit that our mother worked profoundly hard, both as a career woman and a parent. "Yeah," we grumbled, our enthusiasm dampened by her screaming fit that morning when Dad had impudently turned the thermostat up to sixty degrees.

"When it's hot in here, you people just lie around!" she had snapped, impressively managing to not only label us as sloths but distance herself from this clutch of cave-dwelling creatures at the same time.

"But you aren't working," I said to Dad as I Windexed the Formica counter. "Aren't we poor?"

Various financial compromises *had* been made since Dad's unemployment, including cancellation of our membership in the not particularly exclusive Wedgwood Bath and Tennis Club. Val was horrified, but since neighborhood boys routinely tried to drown me in the deep end, I accepted this sacrifice with surprising aplomb.

"Don't be silly," Dad replied. "We're a little strapped, but I'll get a new job soon."

And so it was decided. He was going to surprise our mother. This couldn't go well.

The next afternoon, alone in the rathskeller, I retrieved my Endora caftan from its hiding place and set to work. Summoning all the magical powers of the universe, I closed my eyes, waving my arms dramatically. Our house was swallowed into a blustery void, wind rushing past, the sky closing in, day becoming night as the stars twinkled and snow began to fall. Suddenly, it was Christmas Eve.

As our house settled back into Wedgwood Green, I saw the family gathered around the tree. Mother was opening gifts, chirping with delight and hugging our father, who sat back contentedly and smiled, reveling in his role as patriarch and benevolent leader. She basked in the glow of his authority and commanding presence, a veritable geisha kneeling before Emperor Hirohito. He made a small signal to her and she rose to pour eggnog for each of us as we sang along with the New Christy Minstrels. This was heaven.

I opened my eyes, alone in the basement once again. I was certain that my magic gave me the power to change my family's destiny; now I would simply have to wait for the results.

DAYS PASSED. Christmas approached. Nothing seemed to have changed. I remained steadfast, reasoning that magic of this caliber would need time to develop.

Christmas Eve arrived with a crackers-and-cheese

selection from Hickory Farms and a bottle of Mateus rosé in its prestigious clay bottle. We were strict Southern Baptists, but Mother and Dad rationalized this particular thirst-quencher as symbolic of the blood of Jesus (whose blood was, apparently, pink).

Val and I chewed nervously as Dad called out to our mother, who was scorching the bedsheets with an iron. "Hurry up, the wine's gonna turn."

No answer. Another fifteen minutes passed. We ate. He drank. Andy Williams reminded us that this was the most wonderful time of the year.

He called again. This time Mother emerged from her laundry lair, sighing heavily to remind us of her oppressive workload—those bath towels don't just press themselves. Val and I sat up eagerly, smiling, suddenly animated. We knew that, like a Whac-A-Mole game, the more we could distract her, the less likely she was to decide that her life had gone horribly, tragically wrong.

"Have some wine," Dad offered, handing her a glass of Mateus.

"Cheers to Jesus," I piped up, raising my glass of apple juice.

Mother took the glass of wine and sat down. "It's like an oven in here," she muttered, as her breath created slight wisps of frost.

The opening of Val's and my gifts passed uneventfully. Val gasped with shock at the deluxe set of Remington steam-heated curlers.

"Wow," I blurted out, with a supreme lack of subtlety, "you sure didn't see those comin', did ya?"

I, in turn, attempted to feign award-winning surprise and gratitude as I unwrapped the Matchbox cars and accompanying plastic racetrack.

Val snickered. "Guess this means you'll have to retire the Barbie Dream House."

Our mother smiled, trying desperately to enjoy the moment. This struggle, a heroic attempt to find joy in what was, for her, an otherwise joyless situation, was obvious and somewhat painful to watch.

Dad opened his gift from my sister and me, a shaving-cream warmer. These were the glory days when aerosol CFCs assured that even if the shaving cream was heated enough to spontaneously ignite, it remained whipped and frothy. "Wow, hot shaving cream. What a great idea." He grinned. "I'll have the softest face on the block." Val and I beamed.

Mother raised her wineglass and announced, "Unless you can nail that thing to the wall, it's going back. We have no counter space in that bathroom."

Dad handed Mother a gift from my sister and me. As she opened it—a burnt-orange pantsuit that Val had picked out at Kmart—she paused. "Well, I *love* the color." She smiled. "Very nice, thank you. You kids have such good taste."

Val and I glanced at each other, unsure whether to take this at face value. As Mother placed it on the pile of items that would require pressing (which included anything with a cotton fill), she sighed and mumbled under her breath, "One more thing I have to find a place for."

Our father poured himself another glass of Mateus. I labored to see how many pieces of unrefrigerated sausage I could wedge into my mouth. Val examined her hot rollers with an intensity usually reserved for the contents of a nuclear warhead.

In an effort to remind Mother of the holiday's true meaning, we decided to keep the wine coming. One drink, and Val and I would spring into action, topping her glass off at a precipitously high level that resulted in her having to lean over to sip from the rim like a dog at a water bowl. This constant refilling made it almost impossible for her to track the amount she was consuming and would transform her, we prayed, into Shirley Partridge, groovy mother to a brood of wildly talented kids.

As each package was opened, the wrapping paper was passed to Dad, who stuffed it into a plastic Hefty bag, which, once full, was twist-tied shut and set near the stairs for immediate removal. The bows—which had been Scotch-taped onto the packages—were placed carefully into a separate bag for reuse, since, as Mother reminded us, "You only use the 'sticky' for special occasions."

After what seemed like hours but had, in reality,

been about twenty minutes, it was time for Dad's "showstopper" gifts to Mother. Val and I glanced at each other, two soldiers heading into battle. I closed my eyes momentarily and envisioned myself in full Endora regalia in one last-ditch effort to summon the magic.

Dad handed Mother a large, professionally wrapped box.

"I hope you didn't pay someone to wrap this," she announced. "That's a ghastly waste of money, and you *are* unemployed." She lifted the top off the box and gasped slightly. Inside was a mink stole.

Almost in a daze, she pulled it out and wrapped it around her shoulders, stroking it lovingly. A tear came to her eye. Dad winked at Val and me. Nothing celebrates the Birth of Jesus like a dead animal.

Mother crossed the room and opened the doors of the closet Dad had built into one corner of the basement. She gazed at herself in the full-length mirror that hung inside. As she twirled around, admiring herself from various angles, she declared, "Maybe next year you can get the rest of the coat."

With that, I excused myself to turn over the Christmas album on the record player. Val slunk away to heat up her curlers. Dad quietly began to shave the dried-out layer off each remaining slice of cheese.

"Just out of curiosity," Mother added, "where am I supposed to store this thing? It has to be kept cool."

Dad replied, "Well, it's about forty-eight degrees in this basement. Isn't that cool enough?"

The Christmas tree turned blue, red, green and made its way back to yellow. The only sound was the Ray Conniff Singers imploring us to "Count Your Blessings." Mother took another slug of wine. "Well, it is a lovely fur, what there is of it. Thank you."

Dad, satisfied that this was as high a praise as was likely to occur, summoned Val and me back to the scene of the crime. The final gift was at hand.

With a flourish, he ceremoniously pulled the paper off a large oil painting—*A Winter's Day* by Milton Skudley, a Holiday Inn Liquidation Art Sale winter scene for which he had paid the astronomical sum of three hundred dollars in twelve easy installments. This painting was intended to become the centerpiece of the room no one was allowed to enter unless Billy Graham or Elvis were present—the living room.

As the wrapping paper was shed, Dad, Val and I glanced at one another in anticipation. Days earlier, he had told us that Mother had personally pointed out this painting at the Holiday Inn. Unlike the stole, this gift would be a slam dunk. The evening would end with hosannas and glad tidings as we carried the Hefty bags to the curb.

There was a long pause as Mother surveyed the winter landscape before her. Clouds gathered. The frosty air began to crackle with tension. She rose to her feet and, at a decibel level that could be heard blocks away at the Schnucks grocery store, shrieked, "God in Heaven! That's not the painting I liked!"

All oxygen vacated the rathskeller. Mom turned on her heel and marched off to her laundry lair, slamming the door behind her. The lights dimmed as she plugged in the iron.

It was quiet for a moment. Dad leaned down and picked up the painting. Without looking at my sister and me, he slowly climbed the basement stairs, *A Winter's Day* under his arm.

Val cocked her head in his direction. "Let's go."

Dad marched into the garage, as we followed him tentatively. He picked up a large nail from his workbench and, without saying a word, began to hammer it into a two-by-four stud on one wall. Val and I exchanged puzzled glances. Was he going to impale himself on it? We prepared to spring into action.

Once the nail had been sufficiently embedded, he picked up the painting and, slowly, as if possessing the eye of a gallery owner, carefully hung it. He stepped back, surveying the wall, taking pains to be sure that the frame was level, and that the light from the exposed overhead bulb flattered it; then silently he left the garage.

My sister and I stood there, gazing at the snow-capped mountain peaks of this distant land captured in acrylics, completely mystified by what had just occurred. Finally, Val, who was older and wiser in the ways of adults, pointed out the obvious. "The painting's facing Mother's car. Now, every time she pulls in, it'll be the first thing she sees."

Day after day, she explained, Mother will be reminded of her behavior on this holiest of commercial holidays. Eventually, one day, overcome with remorse, she'll come staggering into the house, sobbing, begging Dad's forgiveness, a broken woman filled with shame and regret.

We stared at each other. This was a side of our father we hadn't seen before. His actions were audacious. Cunning. Shrewd.

We were impressed.

As Val trekked back into the house, I stood before the painting, a faint smile creeping across my face. This wasn't quite the magic I had envisioned. There would be no geisha moments, no singing of carols. But Dad had, at least for the moment, triumphed. And his act of courage and defiance did feel truly magical.

THREE

A Call to Arms

I spotted the new girl the moment I entered the classroom. Stacy was lanky, blond and beautiful, with a smattering of sun-kissed freckles across her nose. She exuded a devil-may-care confidence as she sat tilted back in her chair, her bare feet on top of the laminated desk, virtually daring the teacher to reprimand her.

As someone with absolutely no backbone, I was wildly impressed by this audacious, defiant act. This girl was a renegade. It was not until an hour later, when we were asked to write our names on a sheet of paper and she picked up a pencil with her toes, that

I realized her arms were not lounging inside her mod, daisy-appliquéd blouse.

She didn't have any.

It was a warm September day, and the twenty-four kids in our fourth-grade class were agog at this oddity in our midst. Stacy could write, scratch her nose, even play the autoharp with her feet. Our teacher, Miss Hooperman, elected not to make any kind of public statement about Stacy's physical anomaly. Although kind of her, this simply meant that each of us would now have to embarrass Stacy individually.

"Where did your arms go?" Mitch McKirby asked her at recess the first afternoon, as though she had simply misplaced them.

"I was *born* without 'em," Stacy replied in an uninterested, slightly annoyed tone, as she exhibited a Pelé-like talent with a kickball, sending it sailing to the other end of the playground.

"Do you miss them?" Theresa Tilton inquired, never one to be bothered with thinking a question through beforehand.

"My arms?" Stacy asked incredulously. "Do you miss being pretty? You can't *miss* what you never *had*."

"What does it feel like?" demanded Annette Scarpelli, a big-boned girl with a bowl haircut.

"It feels like my foot needs to be in your butt."

Stacy took aim and Annette fled. The circle of kids

moved back to give Stacy a wide berth. Who knew, I thought to myself, that you could be born *without* arms but *with* sarcasm. Here was a girl who had had a cruel twist of fate heaped upon her, yet seemed to have more confidence than those of us with all limbs intact.

In that moment, I knew: I had to make Stacy my friend.

That afternoon, while Val was in her bedroom recording the day's vast emotional peaks and valleys in her diary, I slipped down to my basement hideout and set to work. Bedspread carefully draped over my body, I imitated a new vertical arm flourish that I had seen Endora execute on a recent *Bewitched*. The bedspread billowed out, obscuring my vision. The chenille seemed to mutate, suddenly, into wings, as I effortlessly glided into the sky for a bird's-eye view of my school's playground.

I hovered high above, evaluating the slightly rusted metal jungle gym, the swings with worn black rubber seats, the sea of kids dodging large red balls that bounced and skittered across the blacktop. Then, gently, I floated down to the teeter-totter, where I found myself holding court with Stacy: she, exhibiting her stumps to the amazement and awe of the gathered fourth-graders, and me, extolling the virtues of being arm-free.

"It heightens your other senses," I declared with

authority, apparently unaware that limbs were not generally considered a sense. "Stacy has the strongest legs of any human being that's ever lived. Step right up and she'll kick you to prove it."

My vision of our new friendship continued as Stacy and I dined alone together in the lunchroom, the envy of the biped community. Later, as we boarded the bus for the ride home, the crowd of seven-, eight- and nine-year-olds magically parted, allowing us easy access to our seats in the high-status back row. We laughed together, sharing private jokes and promising to call each other the minute we got to our respective houses. Stacy twittered her toes at me as she exited the bus, her inimitable wave sparking jealousy and resentment in the other kids. I smiled.

I PRESUMED THAT Day Two of fourth grade would see the soaring of Stacy's stock to unimagined heights. After all, she was unique, exceptional, the talk of the school. There had never been anyone like her.

Unfortunately, this distinctiveness seemed to be veering off course, toward circus-freak status. At recess, kids who had gotten wind of the "deformed girl" gathered around. Most didn't speak *to* her, but rather about her, as though she were a zoo exhibit.

"That's so weird," Ann Ridgemore said loudly. "How do you get born without arms?"

"It's what happens," Shelley Thomas replied with an air of authority, "when your mother drinks Drano."

"Hey, weirdo!" Tim Turkel, the school's most attractive and fearsome bully—and my personal torturer—called out to Stacy. "Where'd you leave your arms—on the bus?"

Stacy pushed her way through the crowd, which quickly parted in anticipation of a fight. "Yeah," she replied, "right next to your *balls*."

I was shocked by her language and tried to choke back an involuntary chortle. Stacy turned to me. "What are *you* laughing at?"

I stammered, horrified to suddenly be the object of her wrath. "You're . . . um, funny. You know, in a good way."

"I could kick you into the middle of next week," she threatened, moving aggressively into my personal space, her fashionable blond bangs tickling my nose. I blanched.

"Hey, everybody," Tim called out in a singsong voice, "Stacy's gonna kill One-Ear!"

Several kids cheered. Stacy immediately turned back to Tim and began to circle him like a lion that has cornered a possum and is debating whether it's even worth the effort.

"What?" Tim said nervously, looking around for support. "He *is* a one-ear. He can't hear out of one side of his head. I'm not making it up." He jabbed his arm into my side. "Tell her."

Stacy turned toward me, then suddenly whirled back around and landed a violent kick in Tim's midriff. He doubled over. Everyone gasped.

"I'm telling!" Shelly Thomas shrieked.

Stacy turned back to me, cupped her foot around my leg and nudged me, as if to indicate that I should follow her. My face turned white. The mob had gotten a taste of blood; now various kids pushed me forward eagerly. Stacy led me to a corner of the playground as they watched in anticipation.

I closed my eyes, envisioning the school assembly that would be called to announce my untimely death.

Everyone would gather in the gymnasium, excited that my murder had gotten them out of class.

"We're gathered here today," Principal Pullman would announce, "to mourn the loss of Eric Poole, who died at the hands . . . of an armless girl."

"You wanna be best friends?"

I opened my eyes. "What?"

"You wanna be best friends?"

I was taken aback. I had no real friends, so Stacy's friendship would automatically qualify her for best-friend status, but sharing this information seemed moot at the moment.

"Well . . . um . . . sure."

"You can help me with my homework, and I'll show you how to kick people," she proposed.

"Cool," I replied, not quite sure if she was serious or just lowering my guard before she felled me with a single blow.

"But if I find out you're making fun of me behind my back, you'll be sorry."

Inwardly, I smiled. Score another one for magic.

OVER THE next several months, Stacy and I became inseparable. We sat across from each other in class, cheering each other on as we brushed our teeth with red dye toothpaste during Dental Hygiene Day, attempted mouth-to-mouth on the blow-up doll during Show and Tell, and played two-man kickball in the open field across from the school during the frequent bomb scares (which, to everyone's dismay, never seemed to result in anything actually blowing up).

Just as my vision had shown, we ate lunch together every day, sitting alone at a table, acting highly amused and fascinated by each other in an effort to assuage the fact that no one else wanted to sit with us. The no-armed girl and the one-eared boy were the freak show of the fourth grade, but we were determined not to let it get us down.

"We're so lucky," I whispered to Stacy as we leaned toward each other and, in an ill-chosen re-creation of

Lady and the Tramp, put the ends of a Twinkie into our respective mouths, munching until we reached the middle. I allowed Stacy to have the last bite, since (a) I wanted to appear gentlemanly, and (b) I didn't really want to kiss anybody, much less a girl. From the corner of my eye, I could see Tim Turkel, seated at the Cool Kids table, pretending to gag.

"They *wish* they could be us," Stacy said defiantly, as she motioned to Tim to look under the table, where she attempted to flip him off with her middle toe (no mean feat, even for her). "Wait till I get him on the playground."

Stacy's house was just a few blocks from mine, and since our neighborhood bordered the school grounds, we had the option of walking to school. I had always been too afraid, since the path was loaded with hiding places for bullies; but Stacy's absolute refusal to be cowed by boys like Tim meant that we now sauntered home each day, laughing and playing with the casual self-assurance of almost normal kids.

Stacy had many great qualities, but unfortunately, a genius IQ was not among them; so I took it upon myself to improve her test scores. Whenever Miss Hooperman's attention turned to the Harlequin romance novel she hid inside her teacher's manual, I would subtly raise one corner of my test to allow Stacy a sneak peek at my answers, whether she wanted it or not.

Normally, my paralyzing fear of becoming Grade

A meat in Hell's barbecue would have prevented such behavior; but I deemed this particular sin forgivable—indeed, perhaps even laudable—since I was helping someone in need, someone whose challenges were far greater than my own. Wasn't this what Christianity was all about? Didn't Jesus help the sick and infirm? I was Mother Teresa with a number 2 pencil.

Then, one afternoon as the bell rang, Miss Hooperman called my name.

"Eric, I would like you to stay after class, please."

I froze. I'd been found out. I was aiding and abetting a cheater, and would be sent to the principal's office for a spanking.

I envisioned the dungeon where Principal Pullman awaited me, a leather executioner's mask over his face as he wielded a long wooden paddle stamped with a series of aerodynamic holes. While Dad spanked me all the time, his spankings were performed with a spatula and were always prefaced by his patented "This hurts me more than it hurts you" speech. They were more about humiliation than pain.

Principal Pullman's punishments, on the other hand, were reputed to be nothing short of horrific, a veritable buffet of butt pain. Rumors were that those who escaped alive could not sit down for months, possibly even years.

I sat shaking in my seat as Stacy turned to go, whispering, "Call me when you get home."

"I will . . ." I replied, "if I can dial."

Miss Hooperman was a kindly, pear-shaped woman who, by our estimates, appeared to be somewhere north of forty and was thus obviously near death. She had never married, which was understandable since she was nearly as wide as she was tall; but her childless existence meant that she channeled her love for children into her students, and Stacy and me in particular. Until now.

As the last of the kids left the room, she sat down at the desk next to mine and smiled. This threw me completely off balance. She had never impressed me as a sadist.

"I have some exciting news for you. You're going to be a Crossing Guard!"

In that moment, I knew that while my criminal activities had escaped Miss Hooperman's detection, God had punished me nonetheless. Crossing Guards were a form of life only slightly higher than Hall Monitors. She thought she was rewarding me, but as someone in the final stages of life, Miss Hooperman had obviously forgotten that this gig meant ratting out your fellow classmates. I didn't even know the real name of our hall monitor; she was so despised that even teachers called her by her nickname, "Wombat."

Oblivious to my panic, Miss Hooperman handed me a bright orange belt/sash combination, boldly labeled with a giant "CG." My very own scarlet letters.

. . .

IN TYPICAL STACY FASHION, she took the news of my impending stewardship of the bridge over a nearby creek with aplomb. The small, slightly rickety wooden bridge joined the school's property with our neighborhood and enabled us to walk to class in both subzero and sweltering conditions, an activity the school district enthusiastically encouraged since it saved them bus maintenance.

"I'll stand guard with you," she announced. "Don't worry, we won't turn in the kids who jump up on the handrails. We'll just push 'em over the edge!"

This seemed at cross-purposes with the school board's intentions, but I had to admit it was a superior alternative to getting beat up for being a snitch.

My first several shifts went by without incident. Stacy's reputation preceded her, so as long as she stood beside me each day, no bully had the courage to actually confront me. A few kids snickered, but I pretended not to notice, happy that for once I was able to use my hearing defect to face-saving advantage.

"Why do you let them laugh at you?" Stacy said, shooting several boys a threatening look that sent them hustling down the path.

"Because I don't care what they think," I replied airily. "You don't care what people think about you, either."

"Sometimes I do."

I turned to her, shocked. "You do?"

Stacy sat down on the ground, her legs bent in front of her as she kicked idly at the tufts of grass with her left foot. "It's just easier to make people scared of you than to make them like you. At least, when you look like me."

WITH STACY at my side, I made it through the entire first week with no major incidents; and as the days wore on, I began to gain a newfound sense of power. Most kids just ignored me, but a few actually seemed impressed, and I began to realize that I might be able to parlay this position into an elevated stature at school, raising my profile from that of Derided Social Pariah to Largely Ignored But Rarely Ridiculed Regular Kid.

Then one afternoon, Stacy's mother appeared at the door to our classroom.

"Eric," Miss Hooperman said, "will you help Stacy with her things?"

I quickly gathered up Stacy's books. "Where are you going?" I whispered.

"To the doctor," she replied. "I might get an arm."

As I stood at my usual post at the creek an hour later, I marveled at the idea of Stacy getting her very own arm. Boy, I thought, the seventies sure are an amazing time to be alive.

"Hey, look, it's One-Ear!"

Having gotten wind of Stacy's absence at the creek, Tim Turkel—who usually took the bus, preferring its captive audience of victims—had decided to pay me a visit, along with two of his partners in crime. I pretended not to hear them and instead imagined Stacy, the now one-armed wonder, arriving just in time to slug Tim and drop-kick his friends.

"Hey, One-Ear, what happens if we get up here?"

Tim and his friends climbed up onto the wooden handrails of the bridge, nearly losing their balance while grabbing on to one another. They screamed with laughter as they jumped from one handrail to the other in a dangerous game of chicken.

I looked on, helpless. "You guys, you gotta get down."

"Says who?"

I pictured them plummeting six feet to their deaths in the creek below, their broken limbs askew, a small trickle of blood dripping from their mouths as they lay there, motionless, their cold, dead eyes staring up at me.

This sunny reverie was interrupted by a flash of Principal Pullman in full spanking gear, warming up by smacking his paddle against a large hanging cowhide as he barked, "Whoever's responsible is gonna PAY!"

"If you fall, I'll get in trouble," I beseeched them.

"Hows about if *you* fall, then?"

Tim's friends jumped down and grabbed me. Before

I knew what was happening, they had hung me over the handrail. I dangled over the creek, my life flashing before my eyes—in a series of brief but poignant musical vignettes—as they screamed with laughter.

A small group of kids enthusiastically gathered at the bridge to watch the spectacle. To their delight, my tormenters began yanking my Keds off while another tugged at my belt buckle.

"Stop it!" I hollered as I tried to squirm free.

They threw my belt and shoes into the creek, then Tim grabbed the waist of my jeans.

"Time to pants the pansy!"

"Do it!" Tim's friends yelled.

"Don't!" I screamed back.

With one rough pull, my pants came down, revealing my now slightly pee-stained tighty whities to the world. The crowd went wild. Tim sent my pants flying over the railing to join my shoes and belt in the muddy creek below.

"You pantsed One-Ear!" one of the bullies shrieked in delight.

Humiliated, I began to kick wildly until they finally pulled me back over the railing onto the safety of the bridge. I tore free from Tim's grasp, pushed my way through the throng and scooped up my textbooks with one dramatic sweep of my arm. As I dashed across the common ground that ran behind the line of nearly identical Wedgwood Green tract houses, I realized, somewhat belatedly, that I had left my clothes in the creek.

"Now you know what you really need to guard!" I heard Tim yell after me.

As I sprinted the last hundred yards toward the safety of our backyard, the laughter began to fade in the distance. Now all I could hear was the pounding of my heart, the rush of blood in my ears, the screaming of my mind in furious protest as I recounted the ways I could—and should—have fought back.

I ran up to the patio. The sliding glass door was unlocked. I opened it slowly so as not to alert my sister. Slipping inside, I crept stealthily across the family room toward the hall, school books in hand. Suddenly, Dad emerged from the kitchen. He paused.

"Did you know you're not wearing pants?"

Although Dad appeared to buy my improvised story of Christian charity ("Tim Turkel fell into the creek on the way home, so I gave him my jeans—and some accessories"), the kids at school knew better. By the next afternoon, the news of my impromptu trouser removal had swept the school, and my nickname, "One-Ear," had been replaced by the cleverly alliterative "Pee Stain Poole."

STACY FINALLY RETURNED two days later. She met me at my house for the walk to school, proudly sporting a new appendage. Her "arm" was not quite what I had pictured. Rather than appear human, it was a mass of steel joints and beige vinyl padding, and resembled the claw that scooped up prizes in an arcade machine.

"Does it look okay?" she asked tentatively.

"Are you kidding?" I replied. "It's groovy! Everybody's gonna want to play with it! How does it feel?"

"Like I'm gonna tip over. It weighs about three tons."

"How come you only got one?"

"I have to learn to use them one at a time. If this one goes okay, I'll get the other one."

We had barely begun our walk to school when one of the witnesses to the Creek Bridge Incident came pedaling by us on his Schwinn.

"Hey, Pee Stain!"

Stacy stopped. "What did he call you?"

The boy sped up, loath to tangle with Stacy.

"What did he call you?" she asked again.

I reluctantly related my tale of woe. By the time we reached school, steam was coming out of Stacy's ears. As we approached the playground, she marched straight up to Tim, who took one look at her new arm and laughed.

"Hey, freak," Tim said loudly to Stacy, "what is that, a robot arm? You a robot now?" He glanced around to soak up the appreciative smiles of those within earshot of his delicious wit.

Without missing a beat, Stacy kicked him in the crotch and he fell to the blacktop. She put her foot on his neck, holding him in place, and slowly opened the claw of her new "hand."

"Say you're sorry." She aimed the claw at his eye, hovering just inches away.

Tim gulped. "Hey, come on," he stammered breathlessly, obviously in pain. "I was just kiddin'."

"Say you're sorry for *pantsing Eric*." The claw inched closer.

"Why do *you* care?" he replied in a tiny voice. "Come on, you're choking me."

"Say it!" Her foot pressed harder, restricting the flow of oxygen until his face began to turn a lovely shade of purple.

Realizing that in his incapacitated and frightened state Tim was no longer a threat, I moved closer and stood with my feet on his ankles, ensuring his inability to move. The requisite crowd began to gather.

"What's the matter?" I said, emboldened. "Cat got your tongue? Maybe Stacy can remove it for you."

Stacy's claw moved toward Tim's mouth. He held his jaw firmly shut, afraid to say a word, making slight choking sounds as his eyes began to bulge.

I was exhilarated. My long-pent-up anger sent waves of adrenaline coursing through my body. Our control over Tim was complete.

"Maybe I should just pants you so you can see what it's like," I taunted.

"Yeah!" Stacy whispered. "Do it!"

Suddenly, the wave of kids parted. Miss Hooperman was running across the playground.

"Stop it! Stop it right now!"

Stacy and I quickly backed away from Tim. Miss Hooperman bent down and helped him up slowly, brushing his clothes off, her face flushed with anger. "What on earth is going on here?"

MISS HOOPERMAN DID NOT report us to Principal Pullman. She knew Tim's history and probably figured it evened the score. For the next few weeks, Tim steered clear of both Stacy and me. There were no threats of revenge, no whispered recriminations. Just a glorious, pouting silence.

Our classmates, meanwhile, were in awe of Stacy's new appendage. No matter what they thought of her personally, they had to admit—a mechanical claw was cool. Every day at recess any number of kids asked for a demonstration, as though she was in charge of an exhibit at the science museum, and Stacy happily obliged.

I'm not sure if it was her possession of this space-age device that raised her stock, or the fact that because more kids were treating her with respect her demeanor softened, but gradually Stacy's popularity began to grow.

Then, one wintry December morning, she didn't show up for our walk to school. I called her house. No answer. She must be sick, I reasoned.

As our class finished the Pledge of Allegiance, Miss Hooperman took a seat on the front edge of her desk and smiled sadly.

"I have an announcement. I'm afraid Stacy won't be coming back to class."

I was stunned. Kids exchanged quizzical looks as Shelly Thomas raised her hand. "How come?"

"Her parents felt that she would do better in a place designed to accommodate her special needs, so she's moving to a different school." Her eyes settled on me. "I know we'll all miss her. She was quite a girl."

Slowly, I raised my hand. "Why didn't she tell anyone?"

"I don't think she knew," Miss Hooperman replied. "Her folks thought it was best if they just did it without a lot of fanfare."

The day passed in a blur of multiplication tables and milk carton art projects. That afternoon, as I walked alone to my crossing guard station at the bridge, I heard a voice behind me.

"You'd better be guarding those pants, Pee Stain." It was Tim. "Now that One-Arm's ridin' the retarded bus, you ain't got a bodyguard anymore."

In that moment, my feelings of loss and betrayal, of humiliation and rage, all synthesized into a reaction I could never have anticipated. I whirled around, grabbed my heavy math book with my free hand and pitched it at Tim's head. The corner struck him squarely in the eye, and he fell to the ground like he'd been shot.

"Owwww!" he cried out. "My eye!"

I rushed over to kneel beside him as he lay on the ground. He was in a fetal position, rocking, his hand covering the right side of his face.

"I hope you go blind," I whispered in a strangely menacing tone. "Then you'll know what it's like."

I picked up my math book and walked away, down the path to my crossing guard station, never once looking back. I was exhilarated. For the first time, I felt empowered. Self-reliant. And it was intoxicating. Stacy would have been proud.

Sadly, I discovered that the buzz of intoxication eventually wears off. As my shift at the creek bridge neared its end, my newfound confidence began to fade. What had I done? Would there be consequences? What if Tim's eyeball fell out? Would he have to wear a patch? Could he get a glass eye like Sammy Davis, Jr.?

TIM HAD A SHINER for a good two weeks, but, thankfully, he retained his vision. And because I went along with the lie that he tripped and hit his eye on a doorknob (the astronomical odds of which seemed to elude our classmates), he developed a newfound respect for me—or at least a grudging acceptance. "Pee Stain Poole" was discarded in favor of a new nickname, "CessPoole," which was used more as a passing, dismissive greeting than a challenge. And most important, he no longer tried to beat me up. There would be no more pantsing, no more threats of physical annihilation. Just the kind of general disregard that he afforded math quizzes and fat girls.

I hoped that, although I would no longer see Stacy at school every day, she and I could still be friends. Stacy was the one person I trusted enough to consider sharing my special powers with, and I looked forward to one day revealing the spell that had made us friends. But it wasn't to be. Her family moved in January, and we eventually lost touch as our contact gradually, and inevitably, diminished.

My magic, however, was still going strong. I may have lost the friend I had so diligently conjured, but by standing up for myself and for Stacy, I had discovered the magic of courage.

FOUR

High Camp

The ominous rumblings had begun weeks earlier, before school had let out for the summer.

Vacation. Arkansas. Fun.

These verbal flashes of horror reverberated through the house as Mother and Dad discussed the details of another potential trip to Fairfield Bay, the resort where they had purchased property the previous year.

A-frame cabins. Pontoon boats. Family togetherness.

"Cut something off," Val demanded, motioning to my various limbs. "That'll get us out of it." She surveyed my body carefully, obviously somewhat concerned about the mess involved. "We'll need a plastic sheet or something, so you don't get blood on the shag."

Her plan actually was a fairly sound one, since these weeklong abductions were plagued with the potential for tragic interactions between Mother and normal people, and were thus far more painful than the loss of any body part; but I had to haggle.

"Why don't you do it?"

She leaned over and took my ten-year-old face into her hands. "Because I'm olll-der," she responded slowly, as if speaking to a slightly retarded four-year-old.

Although "Arkansas resort" is, by any reasonable standard, an oxymoron, Val and I actually did enjoy the large freshwater lake and its attendant water sports; but along with those moments of joy and abandon came seven days of being trapped in a foreign environment with a woman for whom unpredictability was highly predictable. Her inclination, for example, to treat the nice men at the marina like serfs in the court of Queen Victoria was mortifying; and it had come back to haunt us more than once, as our pontoon boats mysteriously ran out of gas halfway across the lake.

"I've got it!" Val said, snapping her fingers. "We'll do it in the garage. Then I can just hose it down." She held her hand up to one side of my head as if to picture me differently. "How about your right ear? You're not using it, anyway."

Magic was needed.

I retreated to the rathskeller for a supernatural session. Bedspread securely in place, my arms waving and elephant sleeves billowing in a rush of fabric about my face, I commanded a respite from these potential Arkansas atrocities.

A flash of white light obliterated the basement. As the bedspread's stringy white fringe came to rest at my sides, I realized that Dad, Val and I had been transported to a stunningly exotic locale—we were standing before the entrance to Walt Disney World, the consummate theme park that had recently opened in Florida. Now *this* was fun.

Photographers snapped our picture as Val and I walked through the gates holding Dad's hands. It's important to look modest, I reminded myself, so that the masses don't resent your glamour and privilege.

Reporters hungrily scribbled our names on pads and questioned why Mother couldn't be with us.

"She's recuperating," Dad explained, "from a fall off a stepladder while she was vacuuming the ceiling tile." They clucked their tongues knowingly. "She'll be fine," he added. "She has a three-day supply of food and we made the vacuum cleaner into a walker."

Another flash of white light filled the room, and we found ourselves checking into our spectacular suite (Mickey Mouse wallpaper! "It's a Small World" on Muzak!) at the glamorous Walt Disney World Resort, exhausted from an exhilarating day of rides and attractions experienced thus far by only a select few. We watched *The Wonderful World of Disney* on television with Dad as we ate popcorn in bed. It was heaven.

"What on earth are you doing?!"

I was slammed back into rathskeller reality by the sudden appearance of Mother, who I had not realized had been in the laundry room. She stared at me, mystified.

"I'm . . . uh . . . cold," I stammered.

"It's sixty degrees down here!" she barked, as she stood holding two pairs of Keds tennis shoes whose tongues she had just pressed.

"Well, it's—it's cool when you're not moving around," I stammered, hoping she hadn't witnessed my carefully rehearsed waving to the paparazzi. "Here, I'm warmer now." I yanked off the bedspread and hesitantly handed it to her.

"Great. Now I'll have to wash this." She held up the Keds. "Like I don't have better things to do."

MY POWERS HAD obviously continued to mature, for before plans could be cemented for our next tragic foray into family getaways, our great-aunt Jinny—a spry, athletic spinster who was our father's aunt—called collect to invite Val and me to accompany her on one of her weeklong camping trips to Roaring

River State Park. Granted, this was no trip to Disney World, but it was that most magical of vacations nonetheless: a Mother-free week.

We only saw Aunt Jinny once or twice a year when we visited our relatives in Kansas City, so we weren't exactly close; but she sent us each five dollars every birthday and Christmas, which was pretty much all that was required to win our mercenary loyalty. Who knows, we thought, maybe we can squeeze some extra cash out of her.

"The kids will love it!" Aunt Jinny barked to Dad on the phone.

"Boy, Aunt Virginia, I gotta be honest," Dad responded, "I'm not real sure you'd have a good time with them. They're not really the outdoorsy types."

"Oh, nonsense," she replied. "Once I get 'em out of that pampered city world, they'll turn into regular Daniel Boones. *You* grew up that way. It's in their blood." We nodded enthusiastically.

"Well . . . okay. Here, say hi to Elaine." He handed Mother the phone. Mother waved her arms, mouthing "No!" as though the handset had suddenly become radioactive and Dad was trying to kill her.

"Oh, sorry," Dad improvised, "she's Lemon Pledging the Zenith." He mumbled his good-byes and hung up the phone.

"You do realize," Mother said, turning to me, "that you won't have TV for an entire week. Can you actually survive without *Bewitched*?" she said drolly, glancing at Dad. "I think the jury's out on that one."

I nodded furiously, inwardly smiling at the clue-lessness of these well-meaning adults. I won't need my beloved television magic, I thought. I'll be too busy performing it.

Val and I ran down the hall to her bedroom to celebrate our good fortune, astounded that Mother and Dad had jettisoned the Arkansas trip so willingly. Perhaps, as highly self-involved children, it had never occurred to us that our absence was, for our parents, a glorious holiday in itself.

MOTHER AND DAD dropped us off at Aunt Jinny's home in the small town of La Cygne, Kansas, population four hundred, where our dad had grown up. Even at the age of ten, I recognized that this place was slightly backward. Although the rambling clapboard house Aunt Jinny lived in had been recently equipped with indoor plumbing, an outhouse still stood in the backyard as a subtle reminder that convenience and sanitation were, for her money, the province of hedonists.

As we pulled into the driveway, Aunt Jinny was just finishing packing her creaky 1958 Plymouth, a two-door monolith with push-button ignition and fins that could impale an aircraft carrier. Jinny was a small but sturdy woman of about sixty, with short, utilitarian gray hair. She was dressed in pedal pushers and combat boots, a fashion choice that aptly reflected her twin personal principles of sensible style and unfortunate taste. Dad jumped out to help her.

"Well, Ray Lee, just look at you!" Jinny barked. "You're skinny as a lamppost." She turned to the car, where Mother remained seated in the front seat as though awaiting a royal announcement of her arrival. "Elaine, what are you feeding him?"

Mother smiled a bit frostily and waved, then picked up her *Time* magazine and returned to her story on the Tricia Nixon wedding. Aunt Jinny shook her head and swung open Val's door. "Hey, kids. Let's get a move on. Gotta get the tent up before dark!"

Val dropped her *Tiger Beat* magazine.

"*We* have to do it? Aren't there park rangers for that?"

THE MID-JULY DAY had already begun to heat up as we headed down the interstate. We had never driven anywhere with Aunt Jinny, so though her car had no air-conditioning, we were too terrified to be uncomfortable, since she was doing ninety miles an hour and merrily took curves (on two wheels) at eighty-five. The car crossed the line into oncoming traffic with such regularity that I began to mentally assemble a list of bequests.

Midway through the three-hour drive, as our fingers began to ache from clutching the door handles in a death grip, Aunt Jinny bellowed, "Who wants a tenderloin sandwich?"

"We do!" Val and I shrieked with all the ferocity of sub-Saharan famine victims, although we really just wanted out of the car. She careened into a Stuckey's for a pit stop, blissfully unaware of the station wagon full of screaming Sunflower Girls she had nearly taken out.

As we gratefully soaked up the restaurant air-conditioning and wolfed down chicken-fried steak on white bread, Aunt Jinny performed the requisite conversational task of inquiring about our lives, since it did not occur to Val and me to actually show interest in hers.

"So, how are things at home?"

This was an opening we couldn't pass up. Val and I began listing our grievances enthusiastically, thrilled to have an audience for our inventory of Mother's persecutions and deprivations. We covered each complaint ponderously, pausing to allow the full weight of our suffering to settle across the table.

"Well," Aunt Jinny murmured thoughtfully, "she is a handful." Val and I exchanged self-satisfied smiles. She was obviously impressed. "Does she hit you?"

"What?" I replied, glancing at Val, somewhat confused by her question. "Well . . . no."

Why, after this exhaustive recounting, was she focusing on one of the very few areas of Mother's innocence?

"Does she tell you she's ashamed of you?"

"No," Val replied, a bit more deflated. "But—"

"And she works, right?"

"Yeah. But—"

"Every day?"

"Uh-huh," we answered.

"So let's see . . . she cleans the house, works all day, takes care of you kids and more or less lets you know that she's proud of you."

"Well, okay, yeah," Val mumbled. "*But—*"

"So what exactly are you complaining about, again?"

IT WAS APPROXIMATELY seven thousand degrees as we skidded to a halt at a scenic spot overlooking the Roaring River. The lovely setting was somewhat obscured by a swarm of bugs that appeared to be hovering outside the car as we opened the door. The mosquito population of southern Missouri had apparently been having a summer-long drunken orgy. It was one thing seeing these swarms splattered across the car windshield as we had flown down the highway;

it was quite another being attacked like a walking umbrella drink.

Aunt Jinny appeared unfazed. "Isn't it spectacular?" She stood, hands on her hips like a petite lumberjack, surveying the beauty of the surroundings as Val and I stumbled out of the car, slapping at our arms and legs like Timothy Leary on a bad acid trip.

"Where's the Off!?" I shrieked over the buzzing din, as Aunt Jinny began unloading the car.

"Oh, for heaven's sake," she snorted, "a few mosquitoes aren't gonna kill you. Once we get the tent up, I'll find the bug spray." She turned to my sister. "That perfume you have on is attracting them. Why don't you go wash it off."

"Fine. Where are the restrooms?"

Aunt Jinny chuckled. "Restrooms? This is a campsite." She handed her a towel and pointed in the direction of the river.

Val and I exchanged horrified glances. She turned back to Aunt Jinny. "There are no *showers*?"

"Of course not."

"What about toilets?"

"Nope."

"How is that possible?!" Val demanded, as though all of nature should have been plumbed during the Kennedy Administration.

"It's a state *park*," Aunt Jinny replied.

"Well, then, where do we . . . 'go'?"

"In the woods. Just imagine you're Bambi—but without the 'hunters shooting at you' part." Our jaws hung slack. Aunt Jinny pulled out a roll of white tissue. "Oh, relax. I brought toilet paper."

Val stomped off down the path to the river as Aunt Jinny began piling metal rods on the ground surrounding a large camouflage green tarp.

"Here." She handed me a rod. "Start putting these together. Let's build us a tent."

I stood staring at the rods as though they contained plutonium. One of the many traits I had inherited from Mother was a stunning lack of common sense. Slowly, I attempted to insert one into another, to no avail. Round peg, square hole. Although recent IQ tests had placed me close to the genius level, I collapsed into a fetal position on the ground, nearly oblivious to the fact that the T-shirt Mother had starched was getting soiled.

Aunt Jinny had finished setting up the gazebo that would serve as our "kitchen," a four-by-six opensided tent that covered the camping stove and cooler.

"What's the matter?"

"I can't figure it out!" I moaned, rocking on the ground, poles in hand, as I waited for the mosquitoes to extract the last pint of blood from my body. GIFTED BOY SUCKED TO DEATH. I envisioned the newspaper headline, below which a school photo would be inserted. (Mental note, I thought to myself, use the fourth-grade one, it's more flattering than the fifth.)

She marched over to me. "Go sit in the car," she grumbled as she nudged me out of the way. I flew to the Plymouth, slamming the door and rolling up the windows as protection against the flying piranhas.

A few minutes later, Val returned from the river.

"The lake is very pretty."

She had obviously had an internal pep talk en route and decided to put a brave face on an otherwise dreadful situation. Stiff upper lip firmly in place, she and Aunt Jinny began putting the tent together as I, still wallowing in tragedy, lay in the stifling car, willing to trade the threat of heat exhaustion for the reality of being bug candy.

Time for a pep talk of my own.

I closed my eyes and, mentally enshrouded in my bedspread, began to picture a very different scene: Val, Aunt Jinny and me perched on large, gleaming rocks around a roaring campfire, merrily toasting marshmallows and singing the Partridge Family songbook, accompanied by a family of deer and one irascible but lovable old grizzly bear. I envisioned playing hide-and-seek with a woodchuck named Stubby, so named because his tail had been sheared off in a tragic logging accident. I let him win, my reward his sweet, bucktoothed smile. A sunny afternoon found Val, Aunt Jinny and me rafting down the Roaring River à la Huckleberry Finn, watching the forest glide by as birds sang to us in harmony from the treetops.

I am powerful, I reminded myself. Nature will bend to my will.

"You can get out now, she found the spray."

I roused myself and climbed out of the car, yawning. I had fallen asleep while conjuring, and in the interim Val and Aunt Jinny had turned this little corner of hell into our home for the next week—raising the tent, setting up the makeshift kitchen and preparing a campfire for the wild boar I was certain Aunt Jinny would bludgeon and roast over it.

Val—who, like me, had inherited Mother's enthusiasm for cleanliness—had, according to Aunt Jinny, been a whirling dervish of activity, sweeping the clearing (on her hands and knees) with a whisk broom after Jinny had informed her that there was no vacuum cleaner in the trunk.

I stood in the clearing, my arms outstretched as Aunt Jinny sprayed my body with sticky bug repellent, wondering if this was how Jesus started his career.

"Isn't it beautiful?" Val said proudly. She had obviously drunk the Kool-Aid. She motioned to our surroundings with a sweeping arm gesture à la *Let's Make a Deal*'s Carol Merrill, as though Door Number 3 was opening to reveal it.

I gazed around. As I began to take in the surroundings for the first time, I had to admit that, although the closest washer and dryer were miles away, the setting was indeed beautiful. Tall, majestic pine trees made a canopy of green that surrounded this perfect, peaceful clearing. Birds chirped. A light breeze rustled through the leaves. The temperature had cooled down to a manageable eighty degrees. It felt as though we were cupped in the hand of God.

"Why don't we walk down to the river, since Eric hasn't seen it yet," Aunt Jinny suggested. As we crossed through the woods and onto the shoreline, the setting sun cast a warm glow across the lake. The water sparkled. "It's something, isn't it?"

Without waiting for an answer, Aunt Jinny yanked off her combat boots to wade into the water. She motioned for us to do the same. Val slipped off her sandals and tiptoed in, yelping momentarily at the freezing temperature of the water. Once I had removed my Keds, folded my tube socks and tucked them into each corresponding shoe, and rolled up my jeans with identical one-and-a-half-inch cuffs, I was ready to join them.

We waded through the crystal clear, shallow water, enthralled by the beauty that surrounded us.

"This is where I feel closest to God," Aunt Jinny said as she gazed at the towering trees lining the river.

The river bottom was rocky, and the sharp stones began to gouge the tender toes of Val and me, whose bare feet rarely touched anything sharper than the shag.

"Well, when you talk to him," Val said as she and I limped along, yelping, "could you ask him to pave this thing?"

OVER A tasty dinner of campfire-grilled hot dogs, greasy potato chips and Coke, Aunt Jinny grilled us about school.

"So, what are your favorite subjects?"

"I like PE," Val replied.

Aunt Jinny lit up. "A girl after my own heart. What's your favorite sport?"

"Oh, I hate sports," Val replied. "But we get to play right next to the boys."

"We didn't get to play sports much when I was your age," Aunt Jinny said, a bit wistful. "It wasn't considered ladylike."

"Well, it isn't," Val replied. "We have a word for the girls who like to play field hockey. It's—"

Aunt Jinny quickly turned to me, interrupting Val. "And how about you?"

"Music," I replied, rocking back and forth in place, my legs crossed. "I like art, too, but I'm not that good with macaroni."

"Don't worry," she replied, "most of the masters didn't work in pasta."

"My art teacher says I'm 'limited,' but I think she means 'cause I don't have the sixty-four box of

Crayolas. When you're missing Burnt Sienna and Cornflower, any picture's gonna be a little dull."

"That makes sense," she replied, patting my hand.

"Oh," I said enthusiastically, "I also like English."

"And he wonders why he gets beat up so much," Val said, rolling her eyes.

I doubled over slightly, clutching my stomach. Aunt Jinny frowned, concerned that Val's comment had hit me hard. "Are you okay?"

I finally spoke the words I had been dreading all day. Although Val and I could stomach eating over a campfire and possibly sleeping in a tent, bathroom needs were something else altogether.

"I have to go."

"Oh!" she said, relieved. "The shovel's by the cooler."

Aunt Jinny had showed us how to take the small hand shovel and dig a shallow hole in the ground, over which we would squat to relieve ourselves, covering the hole again with dirt after we were finished; but this was, as far as Val and I were concerned, beyond the pale. This was not "roughing it," this was a measure undertaken only by the survivors of a nuclear holocaust. But I knew that my abdomen was about to explode, and if I didn't attend to this immediately, the shit would literally hit the fan.

"By the way, I'd tap the ground with it, if I were you."

"Why?"

"Oh, there's a few snakes in there," she said, motioning to the forest. "You can't be too careful."

Val looked up from her bag of Charles potato chips. "What?!"

"Don't worry," Aunt Jinny replied patiently, "they're not poisonous. They're mostly just garden or hognose snakes. Tap on the ground and they'll run the other way. Here, I'll show you." She grabbed the shovel and tapped the ground lightly as she disappeared into the woods. "See?" she called out. "Nothing to be afraid of."

"I did not come here," Val stage-whispered, "to be bitten by a rattlesnake and die with my pants down in the middle of nowhere!"

Aunt Jinny returned and handed Val the shovel. "Go with him."

"I'm not watching my brother go number two!"

"I didn't say 'watch him,' but you can tap with this while he does his business."

Val sighed heavily, grabbed the shovel and pushed me in front of her as we crept hesitantly into the woods.

As someone who locked the bathroom door at home just to wash my face, this was mortifying. Fortunately, Val was too busy slamming the handle against the ground, as though she were beating out some Indian-style Morse code, to notice what I was up to.

"Look for an escape route," she whispered.

"But we can't just run away." I paused. "Can we?"

"If we can make it to the main road before dark, we have a chance," she replied. "Some nice trucker will take pity on us, and we can probably make it home in time for *Mary Tyler Moore*."

AUNT JINNY rose the next morning at six, banging dishes as she made coffee in a dented tin pot. "Who wants pancakes?" she hollered.

Val and I awoke with a start, suddenly aware that we had made it through our first night.

We smiled sheepishly at each other. What had we been so worried about? We slept like logs, we'd both finally managed to go in the woods. A profound sense of pride filled me as I realized that, although nature had not bent to my will, I had found the power to rise to the occasion and magically withstand such extreme conditions.

The day had dawned sunny and warm once again. After taking turns bathing in the river, we devoured Aunt Jinny's delicious breakfast of eggs and canned corned beef hash, chatting up a storm. Maybe this camping thing wasn't so unbearable after all.

"Let's hightail it down to the lake," Aunt Jinny said as she collected the paper plates, "so we can get an early start on our fishing."

Val glanced at me. "Fishing?"

Aunt Jinny walked over to the car and loosened the knot on the rope holding the trunk of the Plymouth closed. She yanked out two fishing rods and a plastic tub labeled "bait." "You've never been fishing?"

"No," Val replied in her most sincere tone, "and that's kinda on purpose."

"Well, today, on purpose, we're gonna catch lunch. It'll be fun."

What little fish I had had at the age of ten had primarily come in a can, so the notion of eating something that had, moments before, been an unsuspecting resident of the lake seemed not only disgusting but a tad barbaric.

"Since you only have two fishing rods," I piped up graciously, holding up the *Mad* magazine I had just bought with my allowance, "I'll bow out. I have a lot of reading to catch up on."

"Nonsense. You can use mine," Aunt Jinny said, handing one rod to Val, who held it as far away as possible, obviously assuming it was loaded. Aunt Jinny handed me the tub of bait. "Here, hold this."

I gingerly took the container. A thin layer of Tupperware plastic was all that separated me from a teeming horde of slimy annelids.

"Oh, for heaven's sake, they're just worms," she barked. We walked through the woods to the shore and sat down on the bank of the river. The morning sun glistened atop the lake.

Aunt Jinny popped open the covered bowl. The live worms were crawling over one another in a tangled, oily mess. Val and I nearly vomited. She extracted a worm and grabbed the hook swinging from the end of Val's rod.

"Watch me, now." She stabbed the worm with the hook.

I blanched. "You killed it."

"That's horrible!" Val shrieked.

Aunt Jinny sighed. She grabbed the other pole and repeated the process. "They're just worms. Living things eat other living things. It's the cycle of nature."

She showed us how to cast the line into the lake. The first time, Val hooked the back of my shirt; the second time she caught it on a stump. By the fourth attempt for both of us, we deposited the hooks more or less squarely in the water.

Aunt Jinny beamed. "See, it's not so hard, is it?"

We had to admit there was a certain satisfaction in landing the worms in the middle of the lake. Now, as long as we didn't actually catch a fish, this whole thing would be reasonably pleasant. We could sit on the bank of the river and sing the greatest hits of the Cowsills.

"Let's play Name That Tune," I piped up.

Aunt Jinny shushed me. "I'm sorry," she whispered,

"but we have to be very quiet. You'll scare away the fish."

We sat for nearly twenty long minutes in silence until a distraction arrived, in the form of a family of campers who had come to fish across the river. The kids seemed wholly at home, baiting their own hooks and casting their lines effortlessly into the water. I saw Aunt Jinny watching them, a slight look of envy on her unguarded face. I caught Val's eye as if to say, "Well, what do you expect? They're wearing *overalls*."

As twenty minutes became an hour, the sun began to disappear behind clouds, the humidity slowly rising as the sky became a mass of light gray.

"This is boring," Val declared. "I should have brought my *Tiger Beat*."

"What is so boring about enjoying nature?" Aunt Jinny replied.

Everything, I thought to myself. Nature is dirty and unpredictable and lacks climate control.

"Nothing," I said brightly, knowing this couldn't lead anywhere good.

"Not if you want to go insane," Val said. "What are we gonna do the rest of the week?"

"Well," Aunt Jinny replied with a sigh, "I thought we'd fish some more, and go hiking."

"That's it?" Val said. "For six days? Can we hike to the mall?"

After ninety long minutes, during which time the

family across the lake reeled in three fish and I slapped repeatedly at my skin, wondering if my decision to be the blue plate special on the mosquito menu actually beat being coated in sticky pesticides, my rod suddenly snapped to attention.

"Finally!" Aunt Jinny crowed. "See, isn't this fun? Now, just pull it toward you gently."

"Wow," Val marveled as the fishing line unspooled frantically until Aunt Jinny grabbed the spinner, "so there's really a dead fish on the other end?"

"No," she replied, tugging on the rod. "It's not dead yet. We'll have to kill it."

Having not quite thought this part through, I guess Val and I assumed that biting down on the hook some-how euthanized the fish and he immediately went to sleep, dying a quick and painless death as his relatives said their tearful but resigned good-byes, secure in the knowledge that their loved one had died a hero. The reality of a wounded fish struggling on the other end of the line was something else altogether.

Aunt Jinny grabbed the pole to steady it. "Come on, you can reel him in." It lurched as I felt the fish's panicked thrashing. As the fish and I struggled against each other, I was gradually overwhelmed by a God-like sense of power. I controlled the life of this aquatic beast. His future was in my hands. And I now decreed that he must die.

I pulled back on the rod, determined to bring him in. I had obviously snagged a forty-pounder. This would be a masterful moment, one I would tell my grandkids about as they sat at my knee, spellbound.

I slowly began to reel the fish in, with Aunt Jinny's hands over mine, guiding me. As the line got tighter and closer, I pulled away from her. "Let me do it."

The fish was now close to shore and fighting desperately to free itself. I am in control, I intoned silently, summoning my mystical powers. Nature will bend to my will. I imagined the jealous looks from the yokels across the lake as I held up my trophy.

Suddenly, I felt a sharp, blinding pain in my cheek. A bee had stung me. I screamed involuntarily, jerking the fishing pole back as my hand flew to my face.

As if winged, the fish on my line took flight, sailing out of the water straight toward us as I dropped the pole and fell to the ground clutching my cheek.

The five-pound trout flew over my head and hit Val squarely in the face, its gills slapping her ear and blood from the gash in its mouth streaking across her chin. She tasted the blood and screamed as if it were her own.

The trout landed on the ground just as the rod that Val had been holding suddenly leaped to life. It flew into the water and was dragged out into the middle of the lake as the fish on the other end raced to freedom.

Val ran to the water and dove in, clothes and all, scrubbing her face violently like Lady Macbeth with bad aim as she attempted to eradicate the fish blood now creating a large decorative stain on her cheek.

"Oh, that is the *limit*!" Val screamed, pounding the water with her fist.

I moaned and rocked in place, hysterically pinching the area around my wound. It felt as though someone had plunged a red-hot poker into my face.

"I've been stabbed!" I shrieked.

"How can you possibly think this is fun?" Val shouted at Aunt Jinny. "It's no *wonder* you're alone!"

Aunt Jinny stood staring at the scene, immobile, apparently debating whether to help one of us, attempt to retrieve her fishing pole, or simply get in her car and drive away.

As I clutched my rapidly swelling cheek and sobbed, the specter of a vacation with Mother and Dad suddenly took on a sheen I had never before considered. At Fairfield Bay, Arkansas, we had running water. And beds. We went boating, ate dinner in the Golf and Tennis Club, and watched the Monica Lewis Trio perform. True, there could be moments of extreme awkwardness—but we didn't have to shit in a hole.

I felt a sprinkle of water and glanced up at the now rapidly darkening sky. It had begun to rain. So much for this magical outcome.

. . .

VAL AND I sat in the tent as the downpour droned on, the heavy rain pelting the tarp. It had been two hours.

"I have to go make a phone call," Aunt Jinny said, avoiding eye contact with both of us.

Was she mad? Disappointed? Humiliated? Had that other family pointed at her and laughed at the woman saddled with the idiots, as they merrily hauled in another impressive catch?

"I'll be back in a few minutes. Don't go anywhere."

"Where would we go?" Val said morosely. "It's like a mudslide out there."

Aunt Jinny was wearing a baseball cap and a slicker as she pushed open the tent flap and disappeared. We heard the car drive off, its engine backfiring.

"You sure did it this time," Val announced.

"Me? I'm not the one who made her feel bad!"

Val looked down, remorse suddenly filling her face. "I didn't mean to hurt her feelings. But I mean, come *on*."

We sat in silence for a moment.

"Do you think she's coming back?" Val asked.

"I don't know."

We began to contemplate how we would find our way home or fend for ourselves in the wilderness if she didn't return. Maybe we could swim across the lake to the other family and beg them to take us in. This would be humiliating, but they obviously had plenty to eat.

"Guess we can count our five dollars good-bye," Val said wistfully. We both began to ponder the staggering loss of these holiday gifts, as Val dabbed a fresh coating of moist baking soda on my bee sting, a remedy Aunt Jinny had shown her how to apply. My face now resembled that of a chipmunk who'd been storing all his nuts on one side.

"Why do you think she never got married?" I asked. Before this week, I had never given her marital status much thought. To me, Aunt Jinny was just the resident spinster. Didn't every family have one?

"Well, I would imagine," Val replied, "that it's not easy finding somebody who likes pretending they're a POW."

AUNT JINNY returned a few minutes later, to our considerable relief, and the moment there was a break in the rain that afternoon, she packed us up and we drove home. Her phone call had been to our parents, telling them to meet us in La Cygne. She was obviously hurt, and our ninety-mile-an-hour drive home was cloaked in uncomfortable silence as the flat

Missouri and Kansas scenery screamed by, punctuated only by the shrieks of the wide-eyed occupants of other cars as the wind shear from the Plymouth nearly blew them off the road.

Finally, in an attempt to break the tension, I spoke up.

"I'm sorry about your fishing pole," I hollered over the noise of the open windows.

She looked straight ahead. "It's not your fault. I should have known better." She paused. "Guess I was trying to make you kids into something you're not."

"That's okay," Val replied, a brunette bull in a speeding china shop. "You couldn't have known we would hate this crap."

There was a long pause. I noticed a faraway look in Aunt Jinny's eyes.

"I always sort of blamed your parents for the way you kids are . . . but maybe they knew best. Maybe you just are who you are."

Was she insulting us, I wondered, or accepting us? I couldn't read her expression, and in this moment it probably didn't matter, because for the first time since Jinny had announced our return to civilization, it was occurring to Val and me that Mother and Dad having to come pick us up early might be a bigger problem.

"You didn't tell them that we were bad or anything, did you?" Val shouted tentatively.

Aunt Jinny said nothing as she piloted the Plymouth

down the highway like an Olympic skier on a slalom course, screeching in and out of traffic as horns blared and brakes squealed.

"Oh, pleeeease don't tell our parents that we were a pain in the patootie," I pleaded.

"Yeah," Val added, trying to keep her long, blowing hair out of her face so Aunt Jinny could see her grave expression. "That would make you an accomplice to murder."

Aunt Jinny didn't take her eyes off the road. "Sorry," she replied with a tight-lipped grimace. "I'm afraid that ship has sailed."

MOTHER AND DAD were waiting for us in the driveway of Aunt Jinny's home in La Cygne. Val and I tried in vain to gauge their moods as we pulled in. Was Dad mad? Did Mother have a gun?

Dad jumped out and opened Aunt Jinny's trunk as Val and I climbed out of the car, sweating. Mother remained in the car, fanning herself with her *Time* magazine, her jaw set. This did not bode well.

"Well, that was really nice," Val said much too brightly as she attempted to untangle the giant rat's nest that had formed on her head.

"Yes," I added enthusiastically, "what beautiful scenery. It was like living in a postcard!"

Val shot me a "don't oversell it" look.

"Let's go," Dad said sternly. "Get in the car."

Dad carried Aunt Jinny's duffel bag into the house as she trailed behind him. She turned back to us.

"Bye!" Val and I shouted in unison from the car.

"See you at Christmas!" Val added, figuring that, at this point, we had nothing to lose by reminding her that we were still expecting cash donations—or, as we now rationalized them, hazard pay.

Aunt Jinny said nothing. She simply waved and disappeared into the house.

Mother waved back, smiling, then set her magazine on the black vinyl seat and turned to us.

"Well, did you have a good time, for the whole thirty-six hours you were there?"

Val and I glanced at each other. Was this a trap?

"Well, ummm . . . sure," I replied. "You know, all things *considered*." Better start laying the groundwork for our defense, I thought.

Dad returned and swung himself into the driver's seat. He pulled out onto the two-lane street.

"We tried to make the best of it," Val said carefully, not wanting to give too much away in case Aunt Jinny hadn't provided them with specifics. "But I mean, come on!"

Mother sighed heavily.

Dad shook his head. I glanced in the rearview mirror where I could catch part of his expression. He was obviously angry.

"You know," he said evenly, "you two are so selfish sometimes."

"Hey, it wasn't our fault!" Val cried. "Nobody should have to put up with that!"

"Well, what was she supposed to do?!" he replied. "When you're sick, you're sick! It wasn't like she did it on purpose."

Val and I glanced at each other, confused. Sick? Who was sick?

"The least you could have done was tell her you hope she gets well soon," Dad barked. "I'm sure she feels bad enough about having to cut your trip short."

Suddenly, it began to dawn on us.

Aunt Jinny had told them a big, fat fib.

There was a moment of silence as Val and I contemplated what she had done. Why hadn't she ratted us out? After everything that had happened, why did Aunt Jinny want to protect us from getting in trouble?

Maybe, I thought, she was cooler than we had given her credit for.

This camping trip had not turned out to be anything like the magical vacation that I had wished for. But discovering that Aunt Jinny—a woman with whom we had little in common except a love for five-dollar bills—had our back, made all the suffering that Val and I had heroically endured worthwhile.

Well, almost.

No good can come from shitting in the woods.

"Can we stop at Schnucks on the way home?" Val said, her face furrowing into an expression of deep concern. "We want to get a card for Aunt Jinny."

"Yeah," I added, nodding vigorously in agreement.

Mother and Dad's frowns softened as they began to see the deep and profound well of compassion that Val and I possessed.

They don't need to know, I thought, that it'll be a thank-you card.

FIVE

Casualties of Warren

Our father's sentence as Mr. Mom had mercifully ended when he landed a new job in the aerospace industry and we became a two-income household once again. I felt personally responsible for his career resurgence, having spent numerous afternoons performing magical ministrations; and my success had precipitated a sea change in Mother's treatment of Dad, from that of Junior Slave to something closely resembling Favored Employee.

Exhausted by Mother's quest for domination over a home environment that threatened to spin out of control at the drop of a bread crumb, returning to work was, for Dad, akin to an indefinite stay at Club

Med. During his unemployment, Mother had allowed her obsessive-compulsive behavior to develop into vibrant and glorious bloom, like a Venus flytrap in a field of daisies. Now, although the daily To Do lists continued—no one escaped her Windex-wielding tentacles, including Dad—her ceaseless battle against the forces of disorder became, once again, primarily hers to wage.

As could be expected during times of war, sacrifices had to be made. For Mother, balancing work and waxing the linoleum often meant that other, lower priorities were jettisoned. These included such indulgent activities as getting to know the neighbors, none of whom knew our mother except as a black-haired blur in a passing Pontiac.

Val and I considered this a blessing, since her unpredictability left us unable to gauge, on any given day, whether her mood would be marked by grim sullenness, howls of anguish or calls to the Holy Trinity for divine intervention. Every afternoon, we made sure to hustle friends out of the house at least one hour prior to Mother's return from work, since (a) we needed time to restore the place to its uninhabited, model-home look, and (b) screaming fits were a type of theater for which we didn't feel our friends had purchased tickets.

In 1971, it was still somewhat common for neighbors to actually speak to one another and occasionally even socialize. As our tenure in St. Louis wore on, Val and I realized that making excuses for Mother was becoming increasingly difficult, so we came up with what we felt was a sexy yet viable explanation. When neighbors politely inquired as to her studied avoidance of them, Val simply explained, in hushed tones, that as a CIA operative, Mother couldn't risk getting too close to anyone. "She knows things," Val would intone mysteriously. "Things she can't tell a soul. If she got to know you, and let something slip, she'd have to kill you."

This explanation appeared to be working until one afternoon when, out of the blue, a large package was deposited at our front door with a note that read: "From a neighbor who cares." The box contained a wide array of tasty, low-rent snack treats: Velveeta, generic-brand potato chips, Fanta soda pop. Val and I hauled the loot into the foyer and began to paw through it, our mouths watering. We had died and gone to white-trash heaven.

This gift was obviously prepared by one of Val's friends' mothers, who were aware that, although both our parents were once again earning paychecks, the only items in our kitchen pantry on any given day were a box of Lucky Charms and a jar of peanut butter. Friends of Val's often came by to marvel at this absence of consumables, and ask whether we were on public assistance.

This led Val—the family's self-appointed shit disturber—to confront our Mother one evening while she was busily dusting a full-length mirror in their bedroom.

"The neighbors think we're on food stamps," Val announced as she bounded into the room, hands on her hip-huggers, nearly toppling the red Princess telephone on its matching red crushed-velvet stand.

"Good Lord, don't those idiots have anything better to gossip about?" Mother replied, generously spritzing the pressed wood frame with Pledge. "Perhaps they should consider spending a little more time trimming their bushes and a little less time sitting around like crows on a wire."

"We're not, are we?" Val demanded with all the righteous indignation of a newly minted teenager. "Because if we are, I can't go back to school and I'll just have to kill myself, and it'll be on your head!"

"Of course we're not," Mother replied as she removed another layer of shellac from the wood. "I just can't have a bunch of junk food lying around." She spritzed again. "I'll be tempted to eat it."

Now, as Val and I sat in the foyer combing through the care package, we debated how to stash the goods.

"She cleans this place like it's a surgical center," Val muttered, blissfully unaware of her own budding sanitation fixation. "She'll find this stuff no matter where we hide it."

"Maybe we should dig a hole in the backyard," I suggested. "She never goes past the patio. I think there's an invisible force field."

But before we could make a move, the front door suddenly flew open. We froze in our tracks, still clutching a pack of Sno Balls and two cans of Vienna sausage. Mother had come home early. Normally, the sound of the garage door opener was our air raid siren, our "All hands on deck" signal. On this afternoon, however, she had parked two doors down to surprise us, hoping to catch us in an act of defiance, like running the heat or using dishes. She stood above us, surveying the card, the box and its contents.

"Who do they think they are?" she thundered. Val and I backed away.

Mother leaned down, grabbed one corner of the heavy box, and began to drag it through the family room and into the kitchen, muttering, "They want charity cases? I'll give them charity cases. I'll invite some bums over and serve dinner on the lawn. Let's see if they care about *that*."

Val and I remained in the foyer, futilely attempting to blend our DNA into the ornately patterned linoleum.

"God in Heaven!!!! Get in here!"

We weren't sure whether she was summoning the Lord to let him have it, or us, but figuring better safe than sorry, we dashed into the kitchen and found Mother rifling through the box.

"What do you know about this?" she demanded, eyeing us suspiciously.

"Nothing!" we both pleaded.

"It was those McDougals, wasn't it?" Mother said, referring to the family of Val's best friend, Vicki. She motioned to the door. "Let's go."

A death march up the street to the McDougals' house ensued, with Mother toting the heavy box like a three-day-old corpse. Val and I knew that our already shaky standing in the neighborhood was about to plummet. No matter what happened, this would take years to live down.

Mrs. McDougal must have been watching from the window, because the front door swung open before we even stepped onto the porch. She was a short, slightly rotund redhead whose hair color—from flaming orange to burgundy—depended on which brand was on sale at Schnucks supermarket. A lit cigarette hung from her lips as if affixed by Super Glue, and she carried an ever-present plastic tumbler of Southern Comfort, which she was known to set down only when adding ice or mixing hair color.

"Hey, kids," she greeted us, the cigarette bobbing precariously. Her smile faded when she saw Mother carrying the box. "Well, you must be Mrs. Poole."

Mrs. McDougal, now suspicious that perhaps this was not the thank-you visit she might have anticipated, nonetheless opened the screen door and motioned for us to come in. Mother stepped in front to hold us back, everyone standing on the porch with no coats on. Mrs. McDougal raised one eyebrow. "It's a little chilly out here, wouldn't you like to—?"

Mother interrupted her. "How much food we have in our home is really of no concern to you or that bottle-blond daughter of yours," she snapped. Val shrank into the background as Mrs. McDougal nearly swallowed her lit cigarette.

Mother was just getting warmed up. "The fact that we as a family choose not to fill our cupboards with junk foods should be immaterial to you and, quite frankly, is none of your business." She presented the box to Mrs. McDougal. "The next time you need to feel superior to someone, I'd suggest you start with whoever does your hair."

She whirled on her heel and marched off with me in hand, leaving Val to mouth a hurried "I'm sorry" to Mrs. McDougal before turning to follow. Val's clever CIA cover was in ruins. Henceforth, the neighbors simply referred to Mother as "that awful woman."

And thus it was with shock and horror that we greeted our father's suggestion that we have his new boss, Warren, over for dinner.

"Are you kidding?! You really want to subject that guy to Mother?" Val asked, covertly attempting to palm several of the bank's hundred-dollar bills as the three of us played Monopoly.

"Look, if I get in good with him," he confided to us as he returned Val's stolen stash to the bank, "it'll keep your mother off my back."

As a mystical wizard, the prospect left me with a sinking feeling, since Mother's social shortcomings were not necessarily limited to those who lived on our block. It was obvious what needed to be done.

The next afternoon, alone in the basement, bedspread caftan in place, I executed a grandiose wave. Up into the sky I flew and, as if suspended by a parachute, swiftly began to float down into our neighborhood, which now resembled a candy-colored nirvana. I seamlessly drifted through the roof of our house and into the living room. This room, a symphony of expensive flocked wallpaper, blue shag carpeting and white crushed velvet furniture, was a roped-off VIP area open only to those with extraordinary access, like the president or maybe Jesus. I hovered near the ceiling so as not to set foot on the forbidden shag.

As I carefully conjured, several neighbors who had never gotten past the driveway of our home suddenly found themselves seated on the crushed velvet furniture, holding cups. Mother entered, an apron around her waist. She smiled and offered the pot she was holding. "More coffee?"

They beamed at her.

"I'm so glad we could get together," Mother said as she poured, squeezing the hand of the woman in front of her. "We just don't do this kind of thing often enough."

My spell was cast.

THE BATTLE PREPARATIONS for Warren's visit began.

The house was scoured to the point that the Centers for Disease Control could have used it to store vaccines. New decorative objets d'art were purchased to give the home a stylish, almost lived-in look. And Mother cooked: pot roast, scalloped potatoes and green bean casserole.

Val and I were dumbstruck, completely unaware that she was able to prepare any of these dishes or, for that matter, that she even knew what a pot roast was. She didn't wear an apron, but I nonetheless took this unexpected homemaking effort as a good omen.

The big night finally arrived. The carpeting had been vacuumed for the final time just moments before Warren's arrival, the scent of burning rubber from the latest exhausted fan belt still lingering in the air. Val was wearing her grooviest Laurie Partridge vest and had spent extra time under the iron, her hair a highly damaged but bone-straight walnut mane. Not to be outdone, I had spent hours in front of the bathroom mirror, Dippity-do-ing my hair into a glossy, side-parted extravaganza, my many cowlicks pasted into shiny submission.

Mother had just come from her weekly beauty shop appointment, and she fairly glowed in a striking red dress, her black hair a perfectly coiffed helmet of waves. Even Dad had dressed for the occasion, his usual T-shirt, Dacron pants and moccasins replaced by a freshly pressed short-sleeved dress shirt and brown polyester dress slacks.

The doorbell rang. Suddenly, Dad stepped forward to open the door while Mother stood demurely behind him. My jaw dropped. Val audibly gasped. The "little woman" role was an image familiar to us only from television reruns. In the Poole militia, there was only one commander, and it was not our father.

As Warren stepped into the foyer, Mother practically curtsied. Val turned to me and whispered, "Where's the camera?"

I silently marveled at my magical abilities. I was on fire. Tonight, all would go according to plan.

Warren Littleton was a barrel-chested, fortysomething man with shoe-polished jet-black hair and not one but two gold teeth. He wore a large diamond ring on one pinkie that would have been ostentatious on Al Capone.

Warren took one look at Mother and whistled. "Holy moly, Ray, you got yourself a looker."

Mother smiled uneasily as she stepped out of reach of his thick, sausagelike fingers.

"Boy, if I had one like this at home," he declared loudly to Dad, "I wouldn't need all those hookers in Vegas!"

There was a long silence. In the Baptist religion, sex is viewed as a procreational duty with no inherent entertainment value, and as such it was never discussed in our house. Mother maintained her smile, refusing to acknowledge that our guest had just dropped a turd on the shag.

"Oh, I'm sorry, Warren, I thought Ray told me you were married."

"I am," he replied merrily as he slapped Dad on the back. He breezed past Val and me without acknowledging us and sauntered into the family room. "Where's the mother's milk?"

As the evening progressed, we came to understand that "mother's milk" was Warren's term for beer, a beverage he consumed with ferocious intensity. Our parents drank only occasionally, and mostly just wine, but on a recent trip to Kansas, Dad had purchased two six-packs of Warren's favorite beer, Coors, which was, at that time, available only in certain states and thus highly prized in the others.

The more Coors Warren consumed, the more he became what would kindly be described as a raconteur, and unkindly, a blowhard. He had a penchant for four-letter words, which, in our household, had seldom if ever been used and thus, when tossed off by him like cheery punctuations, hung like a fart in an elevator. Val and I had long been taught that these words were not only wrong, but could quite possibly result in our everlasting banishment to Hell, so we nervously reassessed the odds on our admission to Heaven each time he let one fly.

Over his first four beers, Warren regaled us with seemingly endless tales of his high jinks at company conventions. He would punctuate each story with a raucous laugh as if to inform us that he had reached the punch line, which invariably included a phrase like, "With a body like that, who knew she was a nun?"

Our mother continued to play the dutiful wife, her subservience a matter of both curiosity and confusion to Val. I, knowing full well that I had had a hand in Mother's newfound disposition, simply smiled serenely. Val wisely whispered that maybe we should seize this abnormally maternal moment and ask for something—but what? A box of Ding Dongs? The new Three Dog Night album? A getaway car?

Mother gently tried to coax Warren onto a new subject, steering the conversation to his kids. "How old are your boys?" she asked, sipping her extra-black coffee.

"Oh, who the hell remembers?" he growled. "They live with my ex-wife."

"Well," Mother continued, determined to keep the conversational ball from bouncing back to sex, "they must be quite athletic if they're anything like you."

Even at my age, I saw this for the blatant suck-up that it was, given that Warren could balance his beer can on his belly and would not require a seat-back tray aboard any commercial airliner, but he was oblivious. "Yeah, they're all-stars. They both lettered in football."

He turned to Dad. "What does this one play?" he asked, motioning toward me as if I were a stuffed deer head on the wall.

Dad paused, and with an uneasy smile, replied, "Warren, he's only ten. Not exactly ready for junior varsity."

Warren pressed ahead. "Well, he's gotta have *some* talent. You think he's a runner? Maybe he'll break the five-minute mile."

Mother gently interjected. "Eric's more the creative type. He likes music and television."

"Ohhhhh, I get it," Warren boomed, sitting back and looking me up and down. "One of *those*."

Mother and Dad both elected to ignore this statement. I looked at Val questioningly, but she refused to meet my gaze.

Warren, who seemed to feel that his joke had been lost on the adults in the room, decided to press his point. "Oh, *you know*," he whispered to Mother in a bizarrely effeminate voice as he fluttered his hands about.

Mother stood, masking what seemed to be annoyance behind a gracious smile. "Dinner?"

EVENTS WERE NOT unfolding quite as I had anticipated. Thankfully, Mother's carefully prepared meal was glorious, which gave us something else to focus on. Val and I reveled in this rare and unexpected bounty, wolfing it down like Ethiopians at a casino buffet, as Warren, getting progressively drunker, stared at us.

"Don't you ever feed these rug rats, Elaine?" he barked. "You'd think you kept 'em locked up in the basement. Although"—he leaned over and whispered to her as he nodded toward me—"this one, you might want to."

Dad and Mother exchanged glances, unsure what to do. I stared down at my plate, not exactly sure what Warren meant but quite sure it wasn't a compliment. Val carefully arranged her beans into the shape of the state of Missouri.

"What?" Warren slurred defensively.

Dad passed him the scalloped potatoes, probably hoping some starch would soak up the booze. "Come on, Warren. Easy does it."

"Oh, hell, I'm just joking around."

"We're proud of our kids," Mother said firmly, a bit of the charm absent from her tone.

"Well, you *should* be proud of the girl," Warren replied, as he gazed blurrily in Val's direction, knocking over his beer, which to my horror spilled onto the powder blue shag. "She's not too hard on the eyes—all things considered."

As Val contemplated this qualification, I grabbed my napkin and leaned over, dabbing the spill.

"Easy there, guy," Warren sniggered, "your head's practically in my lap!"

Mother jumped up and snatched Warren's beer away. "Here, let me help you with that," she offered, her lips pursed into a grim version of a smile as she exited to the kitchen.

"Wow, curb service," Warren commented, winking at Dad. "That's my kinda wife. Bet you don't lift a finger around here."

Dad just smiled wanly. We heard a cabinet door slam.

Mother returned moments later holding a relic of my toddler days, a battered plastic sippy cup. Warren looked up, confused, as she poured his beer into it, snapped the lid on, and handed it to him.

"Thought you might like this, since you call it 'mother's milk.'"

She excused herself and returned to the kitchen, leaving the four of us to fend for ourselves.

Warren smiled hesitantly, unsure what to make of

this. Everyone was quiet, all of us well past the point of being full but forcing down a few last bites in order to keep busy. Dad decided to make one last-ditch attempt to sober Warren up and keep this badly listing social ship from sinking.

"Why don't we get away from these dirty dishes? Let's have coffee in the other room."

Warren, understandably, took this to mean the *living* room, which opened onto the dining room. He rose unsteadily from his chair and aimed himself in that general direction.

Although Mother was now in the kitchen, furiously polishing the remaining silver off the sterling cake knife, her sixth sense for potential trespassing was triggered like a Brinks burglar alarm. As Warren—who was neither the president nor Jesus—ambled drunkenly toward our most sacred of rooms, Mother flew into the dining room, knife held high.

"What are you doing, you *oaf*?!" she hollered, grabbing his arm to yank him back from the precipice of the room where no man dared go. "He meant the *family* room!"

Warren stopped in his tracks, far too inebriated to bother wiping the look of shock off his face. "What the hell . . . ?"

Mother, suddenly emboldened, added insult to injury. "If you weren't so drunk, you'd know the difference!"

She stood there, her arms crossed, daring him to

take another step. Warren turned to Dad as if expecting an apology, an explanation or another Coors.

"Uh, we don't use the living room," Dad explained hesitantly. "Elaine thinks the family room is more, you know, relaxing."

"Relaxing, my ass," Warren bellowed. "This bitch is crazy!"

Val and I remained at the table, transfixed, like witnesses to a particularly gruesome car crash. Warren turned and wove his way through the dining room, the kitchen and the family room to the foyer, followed by Mother and Dad. He silently opened the front door.

"You know," Mother barked, as Warren weaved down the driveway to his car, "my son may not be athletic, but he's smart, and he's creative. The only two words people are probably ever gonna use to describe your sons are 'brainless' and 'incarcerated'!"

Mother slammed the front door, leaving Dad outside with Warren. She stood frozen behind it for a moment before taking a deep breath and returning to the kitchen. After a long moment, the door opened and Dad walked back into the house as Warren gunned his motor, screeching down the street. We all paused, listening for the sound of mailboxes being taken out.

"I probably should have driven him home," Dad mumbled.

Mother paused in her polishing. "He won't kill himself. Evil never dies."

With that, she disappeared to the basement to wash the table linens. She never reappeared that night, probably worried that her outburst had cost Dad his new job.

But it hadn't.

Dad was promoted shortly thereafter. He and Warren never spoke of that evening again. We never knew whether Warren simply wanted to forget that the night had ever happened—or if he didn't remember that it had.

And I was beginning to realize that my magic could bring results I hadn't asked for, but valued just the same. For Mother hadn't been kind to Warren, as I'd intended; but as she protected her son, something more profound had occurred—she had been kind to me.

SIX

The Theory of Relativity

G randma's here!"

Those words, bellowed in a voice that had long since passed Lauren Bacall–sexy and was well on its way to the Addams Family's Lurch, were unnecessary. Grandma's scent preceded her. Top notes of Winstons intermingled with traces of mothballs and kitty litter to lend her annual arrival a unique sense of foreboding; in those moments, rather than *feeling* the tension coming in our household, we actually smelled it.

Grandma Dorothy was our mother's mother, a no-nonsense woman whose every breath was laced with tar, nicotine and opinions. She traveled with three

Zippo lighters, a pinochle deck and her cat, Tweeter, a blue point Siamese with all the charm and warmth of Attila the Hun.

Before this year's visit, I had spent some time in the basement in bedspread-clad conjuring. My magic was needed. Mother and Grandma did not see eye to eye, and for fourteen days each summer, the house was enveloped in a mushroom cloud of smoke and hostility. Mother was incredibly unforgiving to this old woman who seemed to want nothing more than to play cards, read trashy novels and chain-smoke in bed. It was time, I'd decided, for that dynamic to change. With the help of my magic, Mother and Grandma were going to get along.

For my sister and me, Grandma's visits were a mixed bag. The upside was that, since Grandma slept in Val's bedroom, Val got to move up the street to her friend Vicki's house, where they passed the time contemplating the boyfriend potential of various junior high hunks and sneaking nips out of Mrs. McDougal's tumbler of Southern Comfort whenever she was passed out, which was pretty much any day after four P.M. Mother grudgingly allowed Val to stay in what she referred to as the "White Trash Riviera," because it was a less heinous option than having Grandma camped out in the family room.

Because I had few real friends, Grandma's visits supplied *me* with a ready-made companion for two solid weeks, and I reveled in the camaraderie. She lectured me on the evils of the Republican party as we played endless rounds of card games. "Thanks, kid," she would growl as she threw down another winning pinochle hand and scooped up the change from my piggy bank, "you're keepin' me in nylons!"

The downside of her visits was that our mother quickly lost patience with the smog in the family room and the fact that there was another witness to her evening tantrums, and this friction inevitably resulted in a spectacular Pearl Harbor moment that ended each visit on what could generously be described as a low note.

On the morning of this latest visit, Dad warned Val and me that the two women were getting along even worse than usual.

"Your grandmother and your mother both have strong opinions," Dad explained as we prepared to execute item #6 on Mother's list for the day, scrubbing the patio with Ajax. "They don't always agree."

"How come?" I asked, slipping on my personal pair of Playtex Living gloves.

"Well, your grandmother's a Democrat, and a backslidden Christian, so she's wrong about a lot of stuff," Dad replied. "When we're done here, let's pray for her."

Whether right or wrong, Grandma did have a comment about everything. The previous summer, when

Val came home from Vicki's one day wearing Bonne Bell lip gloss, Grandma announced to Mother, "Congratulations, Elaine, you've officially allowed your daughter to turn into a truck-stop whore."

And when she asked what I wanted for my birthday and I told her I was coveting a recorder (a Native American flute), she replied, "How about a *boy* instrument?"

These pronouncements had stung a bit, but Grandma was quick to explain the reason for her bluntness.

"Your uncle Stewart and his hippie wife aren't gonna have any kids," she confided. "So I gotta make sure your parents don't screw you and your sister up." I peered through the veil of smoke and saw that a tear had come to her eye. "You're all I've got."

GRANDMA'S ARRIVAL was heralded by the screeching of her cat, Tweeter, the feline reincarnation of Joseph Stalin. Tweeter understood the inestimable power of fear. She hissed at anything that locked eyes with her, and favored flesh-ripping as a method of gaining the psychological upper hand. This worked wonders with Val and me, who were afraid to even walk by the closed door of the den that Tweeter occupied like a vacationing despot.

"Grandma!" I yelled, running to greet her as she came in. She collapsed onto the sofa and lit a Winston.

"Never again!" she announced in her mellifluous baritone. "I'll ride a pack mule before I ever *fly* to St. Louis again. That damn plane was bouncing up and down like a nickel kiddie ride at Kmart."

I flinched at Grandma's vocabulary and stuck my finger in my good ear, concerned for my mortal soul. Grandma wasn't a complete heathen, but she did savor a good "damn" or "hell" every now and then, and Vacation Bible School had assured me that this was more than enough to guarantee Satan as my lifeguard in the Lake of Fire.

Grandma exhaled deeply, blowing the smoke into Dad's face. "Ray, when it's time to go home, you can drive me back to Kansas City."

Dad, who was wearing a pair of heavy gardening gloves as he carried Tweeter's travel cage, forced a smile, a gracious son-in-law even in the face of godless expletives.

"I'll just let Tweeter get comfortable in the den," he said, as the cat hissed and swiped at him through the bars. "Elaine!" he called out. "Your mother's here!"

Grandma and I waited expectantly to hear footsteps on the stairs as Mother emerged from her basement hideout, the laundry room. One minute turned into two; two into five. The house was quiet save for Dad's creative attempts to cuss without profanity— "Godduckit!"—as Tweeter did her impression of Norman Bates in *Psycho*.

"Mother doesn't like to stop in the middle of ironing," I explained to Grandma. "I think she's doing dish towels."

Suddenly, Mother barked from the basement, "Is that cat locked up?"

"Darn-nacious!" Dad yelped from the den.

"Yeah, she's playing with Ray," Grandma hollered.

Mother entered, wearing her requisite print housedress and curlers. Home was her respite from the workaday world and the rigors of getting glammed up, and she wasn't about to waste slacks and a blouse on relatives.

"Hello, Mother, glad you made it safely," she said to Grandma as they circled each other in a WASP version of hugging, which mostly involved a slight lean-in, followed by light touching of one hand to a forearm or shoulder. In the Poole family, full-body contact was reserved for clearing the airway of a choking victim.

"Barely," Grandma replied. "That damn plane ride felt like a Tilt-A-Whirl."

"Still lighting up the killer sticks, I see," Mother announced. "I could smell it from the basement."

"Yes," Grandma replied. "*Stress* makes me smoke."

"When you get tuberculosis and lose a lung, don't come running to me." Mother turned to head down the hall. "Ray!" she shouted. "What on earth are you *doing*? Get Mother's bags."

Tweeter yowled. We heard a ripping sound. "Fockit all to heck!"

. . .

THAT EVENING, Val arrived for dinner wearing Vicki's crocheted sweater vest, miniskirt and white go-go boots.

"Hi, Grandma!" she said, flipping her long brown hair in a bad imitation of a very short Cher.

Grandma stared at her as she took a drag off a Winston. "I *hate* that outfit!"

Deflated, Val sat down just as the door of Mother and Dad's bedroom opened.

"God in Heaven!" Mother coughed, waving her hand at the smoke. "Is this our home or an opium den?!"

"Elaine, come see what you've done to your daughter," Grandma ordered. She nodded in Val's direction as she whispered loudly to me, "See, this is what happens when the mother is absent."

Mother stomped in, followed by Dad.

"I am not absent," Mother replied, "I'm just not retired like you, so I don't have all day to sit around deciding how other people should raise their kids." She pointed to Val. "You. Pants. Now."

"You people wouldn't know 'groovy' if it bit you in the be-hind," Val retorted as she skulked off to her bedroom.

"Language!" Dad admonished her.

Mother turned back to Grandma. "Could you take your disgusting nicotine habit outside?"

"I'm not going out to the patio. That bug zapper is gonna electrocute somebody one of these days, mark my words!"

"Then don't stick your head inside it!"

Grandma exhaled a lungful of tar. "Why does my smoking bother you so much, anyway?"

"Because you're turning our wallpaper brown!"

"Funny," Grandma replied as she heaved herself off the sofa and shuffled over to the sliding glass patio door, "for a moment, I thought you might be concerned for my health."

OVER MOTHER'S DINNER of green bean casserole topped with crumbled potato chips, Grandma advised the family that Tweeter now preferred her meals in the morning. Since both our parents worked, Val was staying at Vicki's, and Grandma liked to sleep in, I was elected Tweeter's official caretaker.

"You're always up at dawn's crack," Grandma said to me as she passed the Jell-O mold, the flabby flesh of her upper arms quivering in unison with it, "so have at it."

"Good luck," Val whispered. "That cat would sooner kill you than look at you."

Grandma pinched my cheek. "Thanks. I'll spot you some pennies for pinochle."

Dad cleared his throat. "Um, Dorothy, Elaine and

I were talking about that, and we were wondering if you could maybe not gamble? Jesus threw the money changers out of the temple, so we have a pretty good idea how God feels about the subject. . . ."

"How does he feel about the Vietnam War?" Grandma said as she flicked the green beans out of her casserole serving in an ill-conceived nod to caloric restraint. "Seems like that might be something he'd be more concerned about."

"Well, defeating the communists is important," Dad began, "but Proverbs thirteen, eleven warns us against attempts to get rich quick."

"Well, there you go," Grandma replied. "It takes a long time to get rich off penny-ante pinochle, so we've probably got a few more summers before he strikes us dead."

"Oh, for heaven's sake," Mother interjected. "This is not a casino!"

"I'll say," Grandma replied. "You can't get a beer in here to save your life."

Mother banged her fist on the table and stood up. "Until you see a slot machine in the foyer, you will remember that this is my house and you will live by my rules. Is that clear?"

Mother stared at Grandma, her jaw clenched. Dad smiled wanly at Val and me as if to say, "You know how mothers and daughters can be." Or "I wonder what would happen if I plunged this butter knife into my temple?" It wasn't quite clear which.

Grandma turned to me.

"Your uncle Stewart would never talk to me that way."

LATER THAT NIGHT, as I helped Grandma climb into Val's bed, I nervously contemplated my feline feeding duties.

"Are you sure you want me to do it?" I asked as I handed Grandma a Zippo and an ashtray. "Tweeter hates me!"

She adjusted her floor-length pink cotton nightie and lit a cigarette. "Don't worry; since you'll be bringing her food and cleaning up her poop, she'll probably just ignore you. But remember, cats are like dogs. They smell fear."

The next morning, in an attempt to dull the scent of terror, I tiptoed into Val's room while Grandma was still asleep and began liberally spraying Val's Love's Fresh Lemon perfume on my arms and legs.

"I smell Pledge," Grandma muttered, half awake. "Is that you, Elaine?"

I then crept down to the basement and grabbed my bedspread from its secret hiding place. Much like Joseph's Amazing Technicolor Dreamcoat, I knew that the bedspread was my magical armor. If anything would shield me from harm, it would.

As I timidly snuck up to the door of the den, draped in Endora drag, I heard Tweeter mewling pitifully, like a kitten crying out for its mother. My heart melted. Could it be that Tweeter was just misunderstood? I opened the door, bag of cat food in hand, and spotted her crouched under a chair.

"Oh, poor baby," I whispered, "you're just—"

Her trap effectively set, Tweeter leaped out from under the chair, back arched and eyes blazing as she sunk her teeth into my left hand. I screamed like a baby seal, dropped the bag of cat food and fled, slamming the door and holding it shut with my good hand as I shrieked, "She's trying to kill me!"

Grandma, awakened by all the commotion, poked her head out the bedroom door down the hall and sized up the situation.

"What the hell are you wearing?"

I WAS CONFUSED. My bedspread had not protected me from Tweeter, nor had it helped Grandma and Mother get along. Were there limits to my magic, some sort of set boundaries that it couldn't cross?

I pondered this throughout the first week of Grandma's visit, as Mother's reaction to the disarray into which her spotless home was falling triggered the nightly summoning of our Lord and Savior to the basement. Fortunately, Grandma was becoming hard of hearing, and thus tended to assume that these shrieks were emanating from the TV, which she generally avoided, convinced that its radiation was going to burn out our retinas.

"You better develop some talents like that Stevie Wonder," she warned Val and me, " 'cause it's expensive to be blind."

Early the next week, things became clearer. Near the end of another uneasy dinner, as Mother stewed over Grandma's habit of comparing President Nixon to Hitler, Grandma decided that the political point she was making would be more effective with a lit cigarette.

She had won the war with Mother over smoking, lighting up in pretty much every room of the house. But the dining room had always been sacred.

Now, as Mother left the room to fetch steak sauce, Grandma fired up a fresh Winston. Dad sat back, in shock, unsure what to do.

Val and I glanced at each other. "Holy cow," Val whispered.

"Language," Dad admonished her.

"This country's going to Hell and that Nazi's driving the bus," Grandma declared, the smoke punctuating her words like poison darts. As she continued her rant, waving her perilously poised ash directly over the remaining barbecued Spam, Mother returned.

She stopped in her tracks, as though, for one shocking moment, her brain could not quite compute what her eyes were reporting.

"You have no regard for the rest of this family!" Mother shrieked as she snatched the cigarette out of Grandma's mouth and threw it into her water glass.

"Oh, for God's sake," Grandma replied, motioning to the food, "we're pretty much finished here, so what's the big deal?"

"You don't own this house, Mother. I do," our mother barked, dismissing Dad's role in the family finances, which, at the moment, seemed fine with him. "And you will learn some self-control if it's the last thing I do!"

There was a long moment of painful silence as Mother stared down Grandma. Finally, Grandma stood, grabbed her pack of smokes and turned toward the kitchen. "This, from a woman who vacuums the driveway."

Grandma turned back to Dad. "You," she said firmly, "are either medicated, or a saint."

She stalked out. We heard the door to the patio open, the electrical *zzz* of the bug zapper punctuating the evening air. The door slid shut with a slam.

I was torn. Granted, I, too, despised the smoking—the smell, the ashtrays overflowing with butts, the choking from the thick smoke that threatened to suck all the oxygen from the house—but I also knew that Grandma couldn't help it.

"It's all Ava Gardner's fault," she had confided one day over pinochle. "I wanted to be just like her, so I started smoking, and now I just can't stop. She got an affair with Frank Sinatra and I got an addiction. Life will screw you seven ways to Sunday. Remember that, kid."

Late the next afternoon, I waited for Grandma to fall asleep on the couch after *Match Game '73* ("That Gene Rayburn is a looker!" she would announce every day, as if for the first time, and then lose consciousness), then slipped down to the basement.

Bedspread in place, I executed a spectacular Endora-inspired flourish. Within seconds, our ranch-style tract home was lifted up, like Dorothy's in *The Wizard of Oz*, in a stormy whirl of dust and flurry, and it burst into brilliant light.

I closed my eyes to shield them from the blinding rays. When I finally reopened them, I found myself seated in the family room with Dad, Val and Grandma. In this magical moment, we were watching *The Glen Campbell Goodtime Hour*, eating popcorn and singing along with "Wichita Lineman."

Mother marched past us holding a can of Comet, eyeing us with disdain.

"Elaine, could you sit down for two minutes and spend some time with your family?" Grandma pleaded.

"Yeah," Val chimed in. "You can scrub the toilet with a toothbrush tomorrow."

This visual hung in the air as Mother replied, "I'm just trying to make things nice for everyone. You bunch of ingrates have no idea what I go through to make your lives easier."

We each braced ourselves for the rant that was sure to follow. Instead, Mother's demeanor softened. She crossed into the family room and hugged Grandma.

"You're right, Mother."

She sat down next to us and scooped up a small handful of popcorn. "So, how does this song go again?"

AS I FOLDED and restashed the bedspread and turned to climb the stairs, I wondered—was the spell I had cast powerful enough to restore some sense of calm to our troubled home?

As luck would have it, the answer wasn't long in coming.

In deference to the confrontation that had occurred in the dining room, Grandma had begun smoking outside during the day and early evening hours. But at night, alone in Val's bedroom with the door closed, she continued to chain-smoke in bed as she read pulp mystery novels.

We'd all grown accustomed to Grandma's nocturnal habits and had resigned ourselves to the fact that she was a night owl who read well into the wee hours, choking the rest of us in our sleep as the fumes from her nonstop Winstons filtered through the house.

Thus, on the final night of her visit, it wasn't until her mattress was partially consumed in flames that any of us was aware that she had set fire to it.

My bedroom was closest. I coughed myself awake, and, realizing that there was a slightly larger cloud of smoke hovering above my bed than usual, I slipped out of bed and padded down the hall.

"Grandma?" I knocked softly on the door to Val's room. No answer.

I knocked again, then slowly opened the door. A small rush of heat and smoke billowed out. The far side of the mattress was merrily ablaze.

"Grandma! Wake up!" I whispered loudly.

"Whaaa . . . ?" she mumbled groggily. I yanked at her arm to pull her away from the flames.

"The bed's on fire!" I hollered.

At that, Grandma awoke with a start. "Jesus H . . . !" She leaped up and held her finger to her lips to silence me. "Don't wake your mother!"

She ran down the hall and came back with a water glass from the bathroom. She threw the water onto the fire. Nothing. The flames began to lick at the curtains as I grabbed the glass and ran back down the hall to refill it.

"Dad!" I yelled in a stage whisper, pausing outside my parents' bedroom door. "Can you come here?"

A moment later, the door opened, and Dad's eyes widened as he took in the scene.

"Mother-funhouse!" he yelled, running to Val's bedroom. He yanked the bed linens off the bed and tried to smother the flames. "Call the fire department! The number's on the side of the phone!"

I burst into the den where Tweeter was sleeping, completely forgetting she was there. She jumped up and flew under a chair as I grabbed the handset. I dialed the number on the sticker pasted to the side of the red rotary phone and yelled, "Fire! We're on fire!"

A hand suddenly grabbed the phone.

"Thirty-five seventy-four Woodpath Drive, in Florissant," Mother told the operator forcefully. "Please hurry." She turned to me. "Go get the bucket from the garage and fill it up with water as fast as you can."

By the time I'd managed to fill the bucket in the kitchen sink, I could hear sirens approaching. I flew back to the bedroom. Dad had extinguished the mattress, but one of the curtains was now ablaze. Dad snatched the bucket from me and doused it.

"Stay back!" Mother ordered, as Grandma held me outside the room.

Dad yanked the curtains from the rod, snapping the rod and pulling the hardware from the wall. He threw the remaining bedcovers on top and began to stomp on them.

Mother turned to Grandma. "Open the door so the firemen can get in!"

The firemen were already at the front door by the time she reached it.

"It's the back bedroom!" Grandma hollered as they rushed past her. "We don't know *what* happened!"

The firemen dragged the giant hose through the house, hustling down the hall, yelling orders through a chain of men to the ones remaining on the truck. With a few short bursts of water, they extinguished the remaining flames.

The sirens and flashing red lights had summoned some of the neighbors, who now crowded onto the front lawn. We heard footsteps pounding down the hall. Val ran into the bedroom.

Val gasped. "My room!"

She tore around the bedroom, surveying the damage with wild eyes.

"Bobby!" she sobbed melodramatically in front of the poster of Bobby Sherman, her idol, which was now blackened and curled around the edges, a hole burned into his chin where the cleft once was. The door to her walk-in closet stood open a crack. She yanked it open to reveal a rack of smoke-and-ash-covered clothes.

"Look," I said helpfully, slipping into the closet behind her, "they're not burned. Throw 'em in the washer, they'll be good as new. And if not, you can have some of mine."

This was, perhaps, more thoughtful than practical since Val was three and a half years older. And a girl. Mother thanked the firemen for their quick response before she turned on her heel and left the room.

One of the firemen handed Grandma a handful of soggy cigarette butts. "You shouldn't smoke in bed."

"I wasn't!" Grandma announced indignantly to the assembled crowd. "This place is obviously just a tinderbox."

Dad turned to Val. "Go back to Vicki's. We'll clean this up. Don't worry, it'll be good as new."

Val padded morosely back down the hall as Mother was returning with a bucket of soapy water and a sponge.

"Everybody out!" she ordered, as she began to scrub one wall. The firemen carried their hose back down the hall and out the front door, closing it behind them as we heard the neighbors grilling them: "Is there anything left?"

Mrs. McDougal piped up. "Is Elaine dead?"

Grandma and I backed out of the bedroom to give Mother room to work. She tossed a sponge to Dad.

"Well, don't just stand there," Mother said to him. It was one A.M., but they wouldn't be returning to bed anytime soon.

Grandma stood awkwardly in the doorway as they scrubbed. "Well," she announced, "this is just shocking. What a way to end my stay here."

"You certainly have," Mother mumbled through gritted teeth.

"Have what?"

"Ended your stay here. This will be the last time you're invited to this house."

Grandma looked startled. "What?"

Mother continued scrubbing, rubbing so hard she threatened to break through the plaster. "I've had it." Grandma didn't offer a response, but Mother didn't need one. "How many times have we talked about you smoking in the house? How many?"

"I've been going out to the patio ever since your little hissy fit over dinner!" Grandma replied. "Never mind the fact that I'm gonna die of some mysterious disease from that damn bug zapper shooting out electricity."

Mother practically pounded the wall with her sponge. "Do you think for one moment I believe that this wasn't the result of you smoking in bed? How stupid do you think I am?"

"Well, if you didn't make me feel so bad about smoking in the rest of the house, I wouldn't have *had* to smoke in here!" Grandma hollered. "If you weren't such a crazy neatnik, none of this would have happened!"

Mother stood up, brandishing her sponge at Grandma. "Don't you dare blame this on me, old woman," Mother said evenly. "Let me tell you something: you are in my house. How I want to run things is my decision and you have no say in it!"

"Well, someone should!" Grandma retorted. "If Ray won't stand up to you, somebody has to!"

Dad, who was just trying to keep his head down as he scrubbed the soot, seemed to sink farther into the wall. Standing in the hall, I took another step back to stay out of the line of fire.

"I'm just trying to make a life for my family that's better than the one you gave me!" Mother shouted at Grandma. "I don't want my kids sleeping in dirty sheets surrounded by empty beer bottles!"

Grandma looked down. "Stop it. They'll hear you."

"I don't want them to wonder where their mother is when they get home after school!"

"That was a long time ago!"

"I don't want them to get phone calls from strangers to come pick their mother up because she's drunk at a bar!"

"Your father had just died!" Grandma shouted, her voice breaking, her body now slumped as though she had been physically beaten. "I was scared! I didn't know what to do!"

There was a long, shocked silence. Mother dropped her sponge and sank to the floor. I stood behind Grandma, unseen, unsure what to do. Grandma turned unsteadily and left the room, her face flushed. I quickly slipped down the hall and into my bedroom, hoping they hadn't known I was listening.

. . .

A LITTLE WHILE LATER, as Dad helped Grandma settle into the family room for the remainder of the night, I made my way to the basement, hoping to make sense of what had just transpired.

I had never known any details about my grandfather's death, only that he had died when my mother was a teenager. Suddenly, so much of who she was—and who, in turn, Grandma was—seemed to make sense. Mother had grown up in a world she could not control, because Grandma had lost control of hers in midlife. While the ways that they dealt with these feelings of abandonment and fear seemed somewhat extreme to my eleven-year-old awareness, I wondered, as I sat fingering the tattered chenille of the bedspread, if I would have handled it any differently.

THE NEXT MORNING was uncomfortably quiet as Dad loaded up the car so he could drive Grandma back to Kansas City. The only sound was that of a yowling Tweeter, as Grandma attempted to force her back into her travel carrier.

"She just doesn't like being pent up," Grandma explained as Tweeter hissed. "She's a little feline athlete, a regular O. J. Simpson."

"Maybe you should put some raw meat in the cage," I offered helpfully as I stood listening from the other side of the door.

Once Grandma succeeded at her task, and we had finished bandaging her wrist, she was ready to go. Dad was waiting in the car with the cat, playing the radio loudly to mask the lyrical sounds of Tweeter's rage.

As Grandma and I stood alone in the family room, she hugged me tightly. "I'm gonna miss my pinochle partner."

I hugged her back. "Me too. But you'll be back next summer."

I smiled winsomely, trying my best to sell this line, knowing in my heart that it probably wasn't true and that, perhaps, it shouldn't be. The magic that I had invoked to anesthetize her and Mother's relationship had resulted in just the opposite. But maybe, somehow, that was a good thing.

Suddenly, we heard the master bedroom door open. Instinctively, I pulled away and tried to bum-rush Grandma to the door.

"Better get you on the road," I said nervously, "before Tweeter gnaws through the bars of her cage."

Mother walked into the family room, bobby pins still in her hair, looking tired and strangely puffy. She stood a few feet away, her arms crossed.

"Do you have everything?" she said to Grandma.

There was a détente in her voice.

"Yes, I think so," Grandma replied softly.

"Okay." There was another pause, as if neither of them knew what to do next. Then, Mother crossed the room and put her arms around Grandma. They stood for a moment in a rather tentative embrace. A much longer one than I had ever seen.

I stood rocking uncomfortably on my heels until, finally, they pulled apart.

"I'm sorry about the bedroom," Grandma said. "I can send you a few dollars a month until—"

"Don't be ridiculous," Mother replied, waving her hand airily. "Valerie hated those curtains we'd bought her."

Mother walked with us to the door and opened it.

"Well," Grandma replied, patting Mother's hand as she slowly navigated the two steps into the garage. "They're certainly nothing *I'd* choose."

SEVEN

Leave the Driving to Us

Midwest Bus Lines service to Cedar Rapids, Iowa, now boarding."

The monotone delivery of these words probably spoke volumes about the career of the woman on the PA, but they were music to my ears. And they were about to change my life.

Dad and I were beginning the second leg of our annual pilgrimage to Cedar Rapids, Iowa, where each year we drove one of our cars up to leave in the grease-covered hands of Earl, a mechanic friend of Dad's, who spent the next week turning it into a purring model of used Pontiac perfection.

I had never particularly liked Earl, for no other

reason than that he had a habit of enthusiastically attempting to explain the inner workings of the combustible engine. As someone who would crawl beneath a car only to retrieve a Cher album that had rolled under it, I found his explanations so soporific that I simultaneously appeared to be both rude and narcoleptic.

Because Earl and Dad were old friends, Earl performed all the labor for free. When Dad had recently mentioned this in passing, Earl's stock shot up in my eyes, since his generosity was what made these trips economically feasible and allowed Dad and me to stay in the glamorous Roosevelt Hotel in downtown Cedar Rapids—a twelve-story high-rise with an *elevator*— a far cry from our family's typical travel lodgings, where the headlights of returning guests lit our room up like a Broadway stage.

We were now returning to Cedar Rapids to pick up said car, and for my money, the sooner we were on our way, the better. I was no fan of hanging out in bus terminals, since many of the passengers did not appear to be on the best of terms with either soap or the voices in their heads.

Ironically, taking the bus was actually less stressful than having Dad drive, since he tailgated the cars in front of us so closely that the bumpers eventually smoked a cigarette. It never seemed to be an act of aggression—Dad was so laid-back he could pass for dead—but more like a confidence borne of one too many unfathomable escapes.

"Ray!" Mother would scream, throwing her hands against the dashboard to brace herself for the bloody crash about to ensue. "RAY!!"

"I've got it," Dad would reply calmly, slamming on the brakes just as we were about to violate the backseat of a Buick. During road trips to Kansas City to visit our grandparents, Val and I preferred to lie on the floor of the backseat, theorizing that the front seats would provide a cushion against the carnage.

Now, as Dad and I marched onto the belching bus, sizing up the slightly tattered seat covers and the toothless denizens with whom we'd be held hostage for the next six hours, I poked my father.

"What?"

"Maybe sometime," I whispered, "we can take Greyhound instead?"

"Why?"

"Well, their buses are so spiffy."

"Yeah, I guess they are pretty deluxe."

"And I'll bet their customers have murdered less people."

Dad glanced around to see if any other passengers had heard me, although most of them were probably too busy selecting a victim to notice.

"Midwest is the bus line that runs north-south.

They're the only game in town. But at least we get to stay at the Roosevelt, right?"

I would have stayed at San Quentin with Dad. I looked forward to these trips, for they were our special time—time that, unlike our other activities of togetherness, didn't involve annoying contraptions like a weed wacker, a circular saw or my sister. And Dad seemed to enjoy our lengthy conversations, which mostly consisted of my dissertations on why Diana Ross left the Supremes, the importance of snow days to the sixth-grade psyche, and our visitation plan should Mother be institutionalized. Nothing went wrong when Dad and I were alone together.

I even looked forward to our destination. I had spent the first eight years of my life in Cedar Rapids, and had reasonably fond memories of this city, given that its biggest calling card was a Quaker Oats factory and the entire town smelled like oatmeal. My grade-school classes had taken a field trip to the factory every year, and although the assembly line was an exercise in hearing loss, the tour finished big: each kid got two single-serving boxes of cereal, a gift from the fine folks at Quaker Oats.

The resulting sugar rush—as kids tore into their boxes before they'd even exited the sample room— resulted in a spectacular free-for-all that was only quelled when Carl Tompkins's mother, who drove the school bus, blew her whistle and threatened to "beat the living crap" out of every last one of us. It was a much-anticipated annual event.

As Dad and I boarded the bus, we took the row across from a hippie-ish woman with long brown hair. She was wearing a poncho and carrying a guitar. I wondered if she would lull us all to sleep with a medley of Carpenters hits, or if—as I had learned in Sunday school—the guitar was simply where she stored her LSD and Satan-worship paraphernalia. Behind us was an old man who kept fiddling impatiently with his hearing aid, cursing as a high-pitched squeal emanated from it.

I glanced at the driver. He was considerably younger than most of the Midwest drivers I had seen before. Perhaps twenty-five or thirty, he was a small, wiry black guy with a great deal of nervous energy. Why was he so eager to get this trip under way? I thought to myself. As I patiently searched the vast treasure trove of wisdom innate to a twelve-year-old, it finally came to me: he's got a girl waiting for him on the other end.

I could relate. I had recently begun going steady with Alice Larkspur, a pretty, lanky girl from my church. It wasn't her religious affiliation that drew me to her, or her long, dark curly hair, or a desire to go steady with anyone. It was what she had in her back-yard: a thirty-foot-long aboveground pool with a deep end, which catapulted Alice from a 7 to a 10 in my book, and resulted in the understandable need to lock her up long-term.

I knew that at some point I would have to kiss her, but figured that I could stall this until summertime, when the cannonballs and Marco Polo games would make this unpleasant task worth the sacrifice. I was currently in no hurry to get back to Alice, since it was the dead of winter, but our driver obviously had other reasons for wanting to see his girl. Perhaps she had a toboggan.

As we settled in for the ride, I gazed out the window at the gray, icy day. The weather the previous weekend had been uneventful, but today it was sleeting.

"It's gonna be slow going today," Dad said apologetically as he opened his Star Trek novel.

"That's okay," I replied cheerfully. The later we arrived, the less time Earl would have to explain spark plugs. "Hey, Dad, can we get a room on a high floor at the hotel?"

"Maybe. Why?"

"Oh, no reason." Immediately upon our arrival at the Roosevelt each visit, I would grab the ice bucket and head down the hall, ostensibly to fill it up—although in reality, my time was spent pushing all the buttons in the elevator and riding it up and down. The hotel's other guests seemed unusually put out by having to stop at every floor, which mystified me, given the absurdly high quotient of fun. I would return an hour later with a bucket full of ice, explaining that the machine on our floor was out of order, a story that never seemed to lose its credibility with Dad.

As we passed through the city and headed out into the countryside, Dad put his book down and began his favorite ritual: pointing out livestock, something he had done since Val and I were toddlers.

"What's that?" he asked, pointing to a cow.

"A sheep," I replied dutifully.

"And that?" he said, pointing to a horse.

"A buffalo."

The old man seated behind us leaned up to Hippie Chick and motioned to me.

"Got a retard on board," he announced at a vocal level indicating a rather immediate need for fresh hearing-aid batteries. Hippie Chick smiled at me sympathetically.

My face became beet red as I turned back to Dad. "I'm too old for this, you know."

When I was six, teaching me the wrong names for a host of farm animals had been highly amusing to Dad, and highly disturbing to my first-grade teacher, who had called Mother and Dad in for a conference to discuss my apparent learning disability.

"Are you really ever too old," Dad replied, "to have fun?" He started to tickle me.

For me, a feather within five feet would cause an

epileptic seizure of giggles, and Dad's tickling normally sent me into spasms. But today, for some reason, his good-natured torture ticked me off.

"Stop it!" I hollered. I pulled away from Dad.

Chatter on the bus grew quiet. The driver glanced in the mirror. Given the clientele, everyone doubtless assumed I was being maimed, and several people hurried up the aisle for a better view.

"What's wrong?" Dad said, mystified.

I folded my arms across my chest and stared out the window. I was angry. And confused as to why I was angry.

Dad pulled away. "Sorry."

We fell into an awkward silence. Dad picked up his book and pretended to be engrossed by the latest logs of the starship *Enterprise*.

One hour passed, then two. The sleet had become slushy light snow, and now seemed to be turning to plain old rain, which didn't bode well for arriving late to Earl's latest mechanical monologue.

As I watched a guy several rows up swat at imaginary birds, the guilt over my outburst weighed on me. I knew that Dad hadn't meant to bug me. He was simply a blundering adult who, through no fault of his own, couldn't possibly understand the deep and complex emotions of a twelve-year-old.

I decided to strike up a conversation, selecting a tried-and-true topic that I figured we could agree on.

"Did you hear Mother the other night, when she found out that I'd used the bathtub in the hall bathroom? She asked God to strike her dead."

"That bathtub is for guests."

"We never *have* any guests."

"Well, that's true," he said, setting his book down, "but what if there was a tornado and the neighbors' house was destroyed and we had to take them in?"

"She'd make us turn off all the lights and pretend we weren't home."

Dad chuckled. "You got me there. But she means well."

"No, she doesn't."

There was a long moment of silence. Dad put his book down. He turned to me and lowered his voice. "If I tell you something, you can never tell your mother I told you. Do you understand?" He suddenly seemed very serious.

"Sure," I replied with anticipation. He'd never told me a secret before.

He took a breath. "Your grandmother has always seemed to favor your uncle Stewart. And I think your mother always felt like she wasn't good enough."

"I don't get it."

"Your mother is the one who sends your grandmother money. She's the one who calls and writes every week. And she's the one who'll take care of her if anything happens. But it never seems to be quite enough to win your grandmother's approval."

"But why is Mother so mean to *us*?"

"I think she just thinks if everything looks perfect, she'll measure up."

The bus skidded slightly.

"Whoa!" I exclaimed, grabbing my armrest, grateful for the opportunity to steer the conversation away from this now uncomfortable topic. "The road's getting slick, huh?"

"Yeah," Dad replied. "It must be turning to freezing rain."

I looked at the driver's face in the rearview mirror. He seemed unperturbed by the growing road hazard, which made me feel better. He may be young, but this meant his reactions were razor sharp, like a cheetah's.

The bus skidded again. Those passengers who were awake and/or sober yelped slightly.

"He better slow down a little!" the old man behind us bellowed.

Dad returned to his book, and, reassured by his blithe lack of concern, I began to hum "American Pie" as I watched the oncoming cars zoom past.

We began barreling down a hill. Wow, the driver's really in a hurry, I thought to myself. His girlfriend must have a snowmobile.

As we rounded a corner, the bus hit a patch of

black ice. Then, everything seemed to happen in slow motion.

The bus fishtailed, the back half scissoring out into an oncoming lane of traffic as the passengers screamed, the old man behind us nearly imploding my one good eardrum. Before the driver could react, a Ford Pinto slammed into the side of the bus with such force that I thought we were all dead.

The impact thrust the bus off to the side of the road, rocking but still miraculously upright. The horrendously smashed Pinto, however, remained in the middle of the highway, as cars attempted to dodge it.

"Are you okay?" Dad said, grabbing my arm.

"Uh-huh," I replied, breathing fast. I stared out the window, horrified, at the accordionlike car. The windows were smashed, and I thought I could see two people—a man and a woman, perhaps—slumped inside.

"Ohhh, this is bad," I said, rocking in my seat as I stared down at the car.

"Great," the old man bellowed. "This is gonna make us late!"

The bus driver jumped up. "Is anybody hurt?"

Gradually everyone managed to eke out responses in the negative, and the driver radioed for help, then swung himself out the door and attempted to cross the busy highway to get to the Pinto.

I closed my eyes, summoning all the power of my magic.

I pictured a hospital room filled with fresh flowers, and matching beds with freshly pressed pillowcases, in which sat the two victims from the Pinto—a loving husband and wife. They were bruised a bit, but smiling gratefully at their good fortune to have survived intact.

"We must have just passed out from fright," the woman said brightly.

"Uh-huh," the man replied. "I mean, it wasn't like we were really hurt or anything."

"Actually," the woman responded, "I got a nice nap in."

When I opened my eyes, I saw an ambulance and a fire truck roaring up. Traffic had been stopped on the other side of the highway. Firemen rushed up to the car, shouting orders to one another that I couldn't hear. Passengers on our bus crowded around the windows, trying to see what was happening.

"They can't get the car doors open."

"They're breaking the rest of the glass."

"Oh my God, there's so much blood."

The hippie woman began to softly play "My Sweet Lord" on her guitar. I glanced at Dad. Our church pastor recently had informed the congregation that this song was the work of a heathen who believed in the wrong God. Since that time, it had understandably been banned in our house, so I dutifully plugged my one good ear.

No longer able to hear anything, I just gazed at the faces of the people around me as they stared, transfixed, at the scene outside. Their shocked expressions startled me, and for a moment I wondered—what if the people in that car had been Mother and Dad?

I imagined the two of them slumped inside a crumpled Pontiac Catalina. I imagined throwing myself on the hood and sobbing, almost oblivious to the fact that I had messed up the part in my hair. I imagined Val and me meeting our new foster parents, grifters who would insist that we accompany them on a cross-country crime spree.

A lump formed in my throat. I shook my head quickly, trying to clear this horrifying image. Dad is right here, I thought. And Mother is safely at home, waiting for us to return. In this moment, the thought of raking myself into my bedroom every night didn't seem quite so bad after all.

Wait, I reminded myself, the people in that car might be *somebody's* parents. I'd better keep working.

Another bus arrived, which had been deployed to transport us to the nearest terminal. As we lined up to board the new bus, I was almost afraid to look while the bloodied car passengers were carefully loaded onto gurneys and rushed into the back of the ambulance. I took my seat on the new bus and closed my eyes tightly in order to continue my magical ministrations.

In my mind's eye, I watched as the children of this

couple rushed into their parents' hospital room. The son—a creative and talented young man of about twelve who was startlingly handsome—hugged his mother and dad joyfully, as his sister—a loudmouthed and bossy but reasonably good-hearted girl who wore too much makeup—flipped through the TV channels looking for *Bridget Loves Bernie*.

"I don't know how we escaped that mangled car with nothing but a few bruises," the father said.

"Me either," added the mother. "It's a miracle." She patted the hand of her beloved son. "Obviously, someone helped."

A tear came to my eye. They'll never know who their angel was, I thought. But that's okay. I'm not in it for the glory.

As DAD AND I and the three dozen other passengers sat in the dingy Quincy, Missouri, bus terminal, awaiting a new bus to finish our journey, I stared with anticipation at the television screen in the corner of the room, certain we would make the news.

Hippie Chick pointed to the television. "That's a T . . . V," she said, enunciating slowly as if encouraging me to repeat after her, as a voice came over the PA.

"Attention, please. To those waiting to continue their travel to Cedar Rapids . . . as a thank-you for your patience, Midwest Bus Lines would like to offer you a special gift. You may select, *free of charge*, any two items from the vending machines, for a maximum value of one dollar. Enjoy!"

A stampede ensued, as people jockeyed for position, vying for the free Snickers and Little Debbies. I stood back, smiling beneficently at the assembled group. Little did they realize that I had likely saved two lives today. And in doing so, I had been rewarded with the opportunity to feed the masses. It was my personal version of the loaves and fishes.

As I selected a two-pack of snack cakes and a Butterfinger from the machines, footage of the crash scene suddenly flashed on the TV.

"Turn it up!" someone yelled. A skinny male bus station employee, whose reddish-brown toupee gave him the look of someone sporting fresh roadkill, obliged.

I briefly debated whether I should inform the group of my magical intervention, but thought better of it. In doing so, I would be mobbed with requests, and could never accommodate them all in the several hours we had left together.

"—en route to Cedar Rapids, Iowa," a newscaster said as the TV audio suddenly blasted across the room, "struck a passenger car this morning on Interstate 380, resulting in the deaths of the two people in the vehicle. . . ."

The crowd moaned. I nearly dropped my Ding Dongs.

It felt as though the bus had hit me. Dead? I had summoned all my powers to stop their deaths. Why hadn't they lived?

There had certainly been moments in my life when my magic hadn't come out quite the way I had envisioned it, yet it had felt like magic nonetheless. But there was nothing magical about innocent people being killed.

WHEN WE ARRIVED at the Roosevelt, Dad handed me the ice bucket.

"You wanna?"

I shook my head and climbed into bed.

I had been looking forward to watching a special with Dad, a TV concert starring Marlene Dietrich. I had no idea who she was, since in the commercials she appeared to be foreign, roughly nine hundred years old, and unable to sing her way out of a paper bag, but she wore furs and long gowns and was rumored to be a legend, and that was good enough for me.

Dad turned on the TV. I stared at the image of the old woman in an evening gown, and wondered if she, too, would die in a car accident. There was, apparently, little I could do to stop it, if so.

Dad turned to me. "Something wrong?"

"No," I said flatly, turning on my side to face the wall, which, conveniently, was only about four inches away, since the rooms at the high-class Roosevelt were roughly the size of a casket. I was silent for a moment. "I just don't get why those people died."

"Me either," Dad said.

Of all the words of comfort and reassurance I somehow hoped he would offer in this moment, these were absolutely not it. They filled me with anxiety.

"I guess it was just their time," Dad said gently, as he tore open a bag of pork rinds and offered me some. I pushed the bag away.

"But how do you know when it's your time?"

"You don't."

"They were probably bad people, right? So God decided it was time to send them to Hell?"

"We can't know for sure. Sometimes bad things happen to good people."

"Well, that's not very fair. What if those people had kids or something?"

"I guess they'll go to an orphanage," he replied. "Or maybe there's a relative who can take them in."

I envisioned having to move in with my aunt and uncle and five female cousins in Kansas City. One sister was bad enough, I thought; six would be hell on earth. My mind reeled. Could this really happen to just anyone, for any reason?

"God has a plan," Dad said. "But he doesn't fill us in on it. We just wouldn't understand."

"Why wouldn't we?"

"'Cause there are too many things that are just beyond our human comprehension. God loves his children very much, and sometimes he sees fit to bring them home. When we get to Heaven, we'll understand."

I was silent the next morning as we began the three-hundred-mile drive back to St. Louis. Dad beamed with pride at our now pimped-out Pontiac Catalina, its shiny new rotors, pistons lathered in grease, and freshly waxed paint giving it, in his eyes, the look and feel of an Oldsmobile 98.

But I couldn't muster up his enthusiasm. Two people were dead. How is it that the world could just go on functioning as though nothing had happened?

Dad looked at me. "Are you still upset about the accident?" he said kindly.

I nodded as I sat turned away from him, staring out the window at the leafless passing trees, and the few lonely cows roaming about a pasture that was little more than slushy snow and matted brown grass. But I wasn't upset for the reason he thought.

I did indeed feel bad for the people who had died, and for those they had left behind to suffer without them.

But I felt even worse for me.

I had suffered a loss of power, of jurisdiction over the boundaries of my own life. In the past, my magic had always been able to transcend God's plan. When I didn't agree with what he had in mind for me, I had changed it.

So why hadn't it worked this time? Had I not tried hard enough? Had I quit my incantations too soon?

Or had magic somehow abandoned me?

EIGHT

Boys Beware

We are Ambassadors for Christ."

These five simple words were proving to be something of a problem. As a member of the Royal Ambassadors, the Baptist church group for boys, I was charged with a number of vitally important duties on behalf of Jesus, who was apparently swamped and needed some part-time help.

Some of those duties were a snap. At age twelve, I had been a "well-informed follower of Christ" for years, having learned to judge non-Baptists with swift and impressive condemnation. I had a "Christ-like concern for others," particularly those who were stupid enough not to accept him as their personal savior.

I "carried the message of Christ around the world" by thoughtfully assuring my Hindu pen pal that he was going to Hell. And I frequently "worked with others in sharing Christ" by explaining to non-Baptist Christian friends that allowing Jesus into their hearts didn't mean crap unless they also got shoved underwater in the baptismal.

The final tenet of the Royal Ambassadors Pledge, however, was considerably more difficult. Although I had always striven to "keep myself clean and healthy in mind and body," I was suddenly, thanks to Billy Foster, dangerously close to dishonoring myself and Jesus.

Billy Foster attended our church, and our families had been churchgoing friends for years. He was also a Royal Ambassador. Billy had many selling points, not the least of which was his supercool Bible-In-A-Can, a full bible bound into a blue-painted metal can shaped like a bible (which protected God's word from insects, moisture and, one presumes, nuclear holocaust). Recently, thanks to our mutual membership in the RAs, Billy and I had struck up a tentative friendship, and for reasons not quite clear to me, he had chosen me as his confidant.

This special attention was thrilling, if a bit mystifying. Billy was good-looking and athletic and popular. Since the moment I had confronted my bully Tim Turkel several years earlier, I'd worked to develop an air of masculine confidence—no easy feat when I knew all the hand gestures to "Stop! In the Name of Love." Needless to say, I was not exactly Joe Namath. Yet here was the golden god of North County Baptist Church selecting me for friendship.

It began simply enough, with a Royal Ambassadors outing to the local putt-putt golf course. This was apparently an attempt to teach us good sportsmanship and to illustrate that even Jesus liked a little R&R, although this is merely conjecture since the RA leaders spent most of the afternoon ignoring us, huddled in a circle by the concession stand furtively passing around a cigarette.

For me, most activities involving a ball resulted in humiliation and disgrace, yet somehow, I excelled at miniature golf. Billy was wildly impressed, as were several of the other RAs.

Darren Pulaski, the group's felon-in-the-making, whistled as I made a hole-in-one. "Gee, I figured you'd be really lousy at this since you're lousy at everything else."

"Aw, it's nothing," I replied, reveling in the moment as I neatly folded up my scorecard. "But I guess I'll have to bring this home. Mother and Dad have a thing about putting 'em up on the refrigerator."

This, of course, was a bold-faced lie, since nothing was allowed to mar the pristine Harvest Gold surface of the Amana.

"Your parents are really cool," Billy said with admiration, his blue eyes sparkling beneath the bangs of his bowl haircut. "My mom won't let me put *any* of my Little League trophies in the living room."

The bond between us was building.

AT THE NEXT RA MEETING, our leader, Mr. Templeton, a slight, balding man whom we referred to as "The Swoop" because of his dramatic comb-over, set up the film projector for a special audiovisual presentation.

"Okay, boys," The Swoop announced, "today we're gonna talk about some changes that you will soon begin to experience. These changes are completely natural, but the thoughts and actions that can accompany them are *not*."

As Boys Grow explained the process of puberty. Once we were able to get past the hilarious early sixties fashions and haircuts, we found the film highly informative, since most of us knew virtually nothing about sex. Afterward, The Swoop provided an informative addendum to the film by explaining the drastic and permanent consequences of personally pleasuring oneself. I reassured myself that I was not about to indulge in such an act, since blindness, insanity and the A Train to Hell were far too high a price to pay for whatever pleasure might be elicited.

"These changes in your body," The Swoop continued, "might tempt you to want to seek 'physical pleasure' with girls. This pleasure can take many forms, including over-the-sweater touching and inappropriate rubbing. But that temptation is the work of Satan. You must be vigilant and monitor yourself around those of the female persuasion at all times."

I quietly noted with pride that I had never entertained such thoughts about the girls at either church or school and, in fact, found the whole notion somewhat ridiculous. I am, I thought to myself, right with Jesus. I looked around at the other RAs, wondering which of them did not possess my level of personal integrity, and was momentarily overwhelmed with pity for those less Christ-like.

IN THE SPIRIT of joint athleticism, I petitioned Dad to take Billy and me to the FreeFall, a five-story metal slide that had not yet been closed down for safety violations. Shaped like an undulating wave, the slide was one of my favorite recreational activities, since sliding down on a burlap bag required virtually no skill whatsoever and was thus the perfect opportunity for me to show off.

Thrilled to see me developing a friendship with Billy, who was sanctioned as a good Christian boy, Dad was happy to oblige. Mother was just happy to have me out of the house while she sunbathed in a bikini on the patio.

"Take Valerie, too," she ordered Dad. "You know how much she likes the slide."

Val had indeed liked the slide when we were younger, but now, at fifteen and a half, her interests ran to interpreting the lyrics of Bachman-Turner Overdrive while driving around the neighborhood with the car radio set on "stun."

"No, please, she'll ruin it!" I cried.

"Ruin what?" Mother asked.

I paused, unsure how to answer this or, for that matter, even put what I was feeling into words; but Dad saved the day with an unconsciously prescient remark.

"Oh, I get it—you don't want some *girl* along." He winked.

Our Saturday afternoon outing began with chili dogs and fries from the Der Wienerschnitzel restaurant directly across the street from the slide. It was almost difficult for Billy and me to enjoy our nutrition-free feast as we sat gazing with anticipation at the behemoth that would soon hold our lives in its hands.

"How fast do you think they're going?" Billy asked excitedly, a dab of chili tickling the cleft in his chin, as he watched kids rocketing down the metal monster.

"Well," I replied, the wisdom of dozens of past rides informing my answer, "I'd say around a hundred miles an hour." Dad thoughtfully kept his mouth shut, nodding in sage agreement.

Billy whistled. "Wowwww." He jumped up. "I'll race ya!"

We flew up the stairs to the top of the slide, where the high winds that threatened to blow riders off the open-air platform helped ease the heat from the sizzling metal. As we breathlessly reached the pinnacle, holding on to the railings to avoid toppling over the edge, the bored, acne-ridden teenager who manned the FreeFall pointed in the vague direction of a stack of burlap potato bags.

Taking the lead, I snatched a bag and tossed it nonchalantly onto the starting line of a lane. Grabbing the metal pole that hung above the lanes, I swung myself onto the top of the bag. As I held on to the pole, Billy mimicked my actions, jumping into the lane next to me.

"Ready, set, go!" I yelled, pushing off as hard as I could, using the pole as leverage, as Billy followed suit. We flew down the slide, screaming with a combination of abandon and fear, since it was possible to (a) break any number of bones by slipping off your bag and tumbling head over heels downhill for a hundred yards, or (b) suffer impressive third-degree burns on any limb that momentarily touched the searing-hot sheet metal.

Having learned—the hard way—the power of aerodynamics from previous rides, I tucked my head down and lifted my heels off the bag to eliminate drag; and as we hit the home stretch, I slid to a stop well ahead of Billy. He grinned disarmingly at me and jumped up, ready for another run.

"Hey, let's ride together this time. I want you to show me how you went so fast."

I felt a sudden rush of euphoria at Billy's compliment.

"We'll go faster," I whispered as we climbed onto one bag together, "if you sit really close."

The teenager manning the slide snorted. "What, you can't find a chick?"

"Course we can," I replied defensively. "But this is about technique."

The teen rolled his eyes.

"Yeah, man," Billy piped up. "We're gonna rock this thing!"

He sat down behind me, his legs straddling my sides, careful not to actually touch me—but it didn't matter. As we flew down the slide, scenery screaming past us, the ride seemed to occur in dreamy slow motion. Every shift in our body weight, every undulation of the steel was a thrilling moment, Billy's whoops echoing in my good ear like a chorus of angels.

"That was pretty good," I announced as we sailed to a stop, "but I think we need to try it again."

I CONTINUED to handle the temptation of girls with aplomb. Never giving in to "pleasures of the female," as The Swoop called them, I chose instead to focus on Billy, thinking about him constantly and plotting ways to spend time with him.

At the next RA meeting, as The Swoop set up the film projector for another A/V presentation, I leaned over to Billy. "Hey, I'm gonna have a sleepover at my house Friday night. You wanna come? We've got a Ping-Pong table *and* a pool table!"

Billy's face lit up. "Cool! We can watch *The Midnight Special,* and I'll bring my Jarts!"

The notion of playing with giant lawn darts in the dark seemed ill advised at best, and I knew that we didn't dare risk tracking dirt inside, but where Billy was concerned, I was up for anything.

"Great!"

The Swoop cleared his throat. "Today, boys, we're going to talk about something very dangerous and pernicious. Do you know what a mortal sin is?" Several hands shot up. "Have you ever wanted to be physically 'close' to another boy?"

"Ewww!" several kids hollered as others tittered. He turned on the projector.

Boys Beware carefully outlined the sick and perverse nature of the homosexual. A sickness "that is not visible like smallpox, but no less dangerous and contagious—a sickness of the mind." It dramatized the horrific penalties anyone who consorted with such individuals would pay, and warned us, "One never knows when the homosexual is about. They can appear normal; and it may be too late when you discover they are mentally ill."

I froze in my seat. Beads of sweat began to form on my brow. Dear God. The feelings I was having for Billy seemed to mirror those of the kid in *Boys Beware*. Had I been lured into the charismatic sphere of a deranged person? Was Billy an unwitting minion of the Devil? I would not even be having these feelings were it not for him, and here he was, attempting to lead me down the path to destruction. He had always seemed so jocular and innocent, but as The Swoop explained after the movie was over, demons, like homosexuals, could walk in the clothes of a normal man. They could be attractive, fun-loving, personable. They could have a bowl haircut and athletic ability and a disarming grin.

In that moment, the knowledge of what I must do struck me like a lightning bolt: in order to save myself and be an Ambassador for Christ, I would have to save Billy.

. . .

ALTHOUGH I STILL referred to my power as magic, I had recently come to understand that my magical gift emanated from God, and that the kind of magic I had originally envisioned as an eight-year-old was, in reality, a black art. The Swoop had educated me about this during an RA meeting when Darren Pulaski pulled out a book he had found called *The Bhagavad Gita,* which had lots of weird, flowery pictures of guys with halos.

"That book," The Swoop announced, snatching it from Darren's hand and depositing it in the wastebasket, "is an abomination."

"Hey!" Darren yelled, peeved. "I found that in a Dumpster!"

"And that's where it should have stayed," The Swoop replied. "That's the owner's manual of the Hare Krishnas, those weirdos with the shaved heads."

"Why do they shave their heads?" I asked.

"They're just saving time," he replied. "Their hair's gonna burn off anyway when they land in Hell." We all nodded seriously, digesting this important information. "Don't ever mess around with the occult."

"What's the occult?" I asked.

"It's Ouija boards, the sacrifice of babies, stuff like that. You know, witchcraft. But there is a good kind of magic, too, where cripples are healed and water is turned into wine—but that magic is really the miracles that flow from Christ."

It was an aha moment. What I had long believed was "magic" was actually the power of Christ flowing through me. It wasn't *my* magical power, it was Jesus'—I was merely the willing conduit.

Provided that conduit was still open. The bus accident had caused me, for the first time, to question my ability to summon this power at will.

But I was an Ambassador for Christ, I reminded myself. And I had been chosen to perform a miracle on his behalf. Surely that power would be mine for the taking.

Because after all, he was calling upon me to save Billy's soul.

SINCE I WAS now twelve—almost pubescent, practically an adult—my days of Endora-style posturing were over. The bedspread was the costume of a child, and draping it over my body at this age would be weird and sort of girly. So I now chose a far more sophisticated approach: simply clutching it to me, like Linus from *Peanuts*.

I waited to cast my spell until Monday afternoon when Mother and Dad were at work. Val had recently lied about her age in order to land a part-time job as a maid at the Sands Motel, where she could indulge her growing passion for cleanliness by scrubbing the tile grout with dental instruments.

The bedspread—carefully stashed behind the green mohair recliner in the basement—awaited my beckoning. It fairly glowed with energy as I pulled it out and shook it to remove the dust that had accumulated since my last incantation. The fabric had developed a few wrinkles, so I postponed my conjuring just long enough to give it a proper and well-deserved pressing, taking pains not to scorch any of its supernatural force.

I took a deep breath as I held the warm, wrinkle-free material to my face. In my mind's eye, the bedspread seemed to drift from my hands, and I watched with fascination as it moved to the center of the room and began to whirl in place. Slowly, it rose up, as though a figure were forming beneath it. The figure grew taller and taller until, with a sudden *whoosh*, the blanket lifted away to reveal Billy, in all his twelve-year-old glory, standing before me wearing a fringed suede jacket, Toughskins and Keds. I gazed up at him with admiration. He could be a Sears catalog model.

Immediately I blessed his tortured soul and began to pray over him, gently waving my arms around his form to cleanse him of this desire to tempt others. He smiled his broad grin, and I felt a rush of love and sympathy for this boy who seemed to be totally unaware of the evil that lurked within him. With God's help, I will restore his righteousness, I thought to myself, as I placed my arms securely around him to envelop him in magical healing energy.

We stayed in this position for some time, my Christ-force flowing into Billy, his soul being repaired, God's will being done. As I finally began to pull away from him, breaking the blissful bond, Billy whispered, "Thank you," and the bedspread floated down upon him. As my vision continued, it once again began to whirl, the atmosphere charged with electricity, and a new figure began to form beneath it. It lifted away to reveal my former bully Tim, whose face lit up at the prospect of my healing energy. He awaited me with outstretched arms. I must minister to all who ask, I thought to myself. With power comes responsibility.

I WAS UNDERSTANDABLY nervous about the prospect of Billy seeing the inner workings of our family during an all-night sleepover, but the cleansing we needed to do together was now vitally important, so I had little choice but to risk it.

As the school week slowly progressed, I spent every afternoon in the rathskeller in dual magical medita-tions: preparing for the moment when I would cast out the demon from Billy's soul, and attempting to ensure that this event would not be ruined by an impromptu performance of Mother's one-woman tour de force, *"Why, God, why are there footprints in this shag?!"*

I laid out various outfits, debating which was most appropriate for an exorcism. I selected music for the occasion from the soundtrack to *Jesus Christ Superstar*, searching for the perfect underscore for that critical moment of demonic confrontation, including the show's big hit, "I Don't Know How to Love Him," the irony of which was lost on me. I experimented with various hairstyles in an effort to create the most flattering look for someone of my holy stature. I sharpened my skill level at Ping-Pong and pool.

Finally, I was ready.

I TIMED Billy's arrival to coincide with Mother's nightly segue into the bedroom, which typically occurred shortly after her arrival home from work. After a concise examination of the family's refusal to live up to even the most minimal standards of home hygiene, she would retreat into the bedroom, defeated, finally emerging some time later in her tattered housedress and curlers to force down some Triscuits and a celery stalk at the dinner table.

The doorbell rang several short minutes after the finale of tonight's Poole Family Failures Recap. With Mother ensconced in the bedroom, I took a deep breath to shake off the massive disappointment I had caused and ran to answer the door. Billy was standing there in a "Keep on Truckin'" T-shirt and jeans, the bright blue of the iron-on matching his bright blue eyes. He held a giant box of Jarts. I yanked him off the front porch as Mrs. Foster waved good-bye from their paneled nine-seater station wagon.

"What do you wanna play first," I said excitedly, "Ping-Pong or pool?"

"I was thinking Jarts," Billy replied, "before it gets too dark." He opened the box to reveal gleaming metal darts large enough to fell Bigfoot.

"Oh, sorry," I said hurriedly, eager to get him to the safety of the basement, "we'll have to wait until tomorrow. Dad just watered the lawn, and Mother said if we slip and kill ourselves she's not driving us to the mortuary."

I pushed Billy through the family room, passing Val, who was on her way out for an evening of trolling the neighborhood with her friend Vicki. She was wearing purple hot pants and wedgies, and as she passed, she held her finger to her lips to shush us, knowing that Mother and Dad would have a fit if they saw her outfit.

"You owe me," I whispered.

Billy turned to watch her leave the room. "Man, your sister's pretty."

My eyes rolled into the back of my head. "Gross!" I pushed him nervously toward the stairs.

"What's the big rush?" he asked.

This night is not about my stupid teenage sister, I wanted to say. Or about your witnessing Mother doing her impression of Bag Lady Macbeth. This night is about a healing that has to happen. God has commanded it.

"Oh, I'm just excited," I replied as I bum-rushed him down the stairs. "The basement's where all the fun is. I hang out there a lot."

We descended the stairs into the rathskeller and I picked up the Ping-Pong paddles and handed one to Billy. "So where are the other guys?" Billy asked.

"What other guys?"

"You said this was a party. So who else is coming?"

The blood began to drain from my face. "Umm, nobody. I thought it would be fun if it was just, you know . . ."

"Oh, that's cool," he said, bouncing one of the egg-shell balls on the paddle as he surveyed the surroundings. "Man," he whistled, "nine couches?"

I beamed. He wanted to be alone with me! My face flushed with pride and confidence. Tonight, we would do God's work.

TWO HOURS PASSED as we alternated between furiously competitive games of Ping-Pong and pool. For some odd reason, although I had played hundreds of times and he had never played before, Billy was beating me.

"You think you're so hot?" I said challengingly as I laid my cue stick on the pool table. "Bet I'm a better wrestler!"

"Oh, yeah?" he barked.

Billy grabbed me and threw me to the ground. We began to roll around, getting rug burns from the cheap industrial carpeting as we both struggled for dominance. Fortunately, I was bigger than Billy and was able to straddle him fairly quickly, pinning his arms and legs down. He tried to throw me off, to no avail. I sat on his torso, holding him down, lingering in the moment. It was important for me to establish control so that the demon inside Billy would know who was boss.

"All right, I give!" he hollered.

I leaned over, my face mere inches from his. "Who's Dick the Bruiser?" I demanded, referring to a pro wrestler whose matches I had spent hours watching with my grandmother.

"You are!"

"Say it like you mean it!" I barked.

"You are! You're Dick the Bruiser!" he yelled. "Now let me up!"

I remained atop him, refusing to move, focusing my mind's eye on the exorcism to come.

"What are you doing? Let! Me! Up!" Billy bellowed, annoyed. He pushed as hard as he could, finally throwing me off with a heave. I tumbled backward as he jumped to his feet, brushing himself off with an odd measure of anger and disgust.

Before I was able to formulate an excuse for holding him down, we were startled by a voice.

"Soup's on." We turned to find Dad standing at the foot of the stairs holding a pizza box and a pitcher of Tang, staring at us curiously. I ran to grab the food.

"Hi, Mr. Poole," Billy called out, his voice still reflecting his annoyance.

"Hi, Billy." He turned to me. "Everything okay?"

"Yeah, sure, why?" I replied in a rush of words. "No problems here. Boy, are we hungry. Is this sausage? I hope so. Thanks for the Tang."

"Spread these out on the floor," Dad whispered to me, handing me a roll of paper towels. "You get any crumbs on that carpet and your mother will have a stroke." I nodded with tacit understanding. Must not poke the bear.

"Have fun." Dad ambled up the stairs, glancing back at us.

We took a break to stuff our faces and watch *Sanford and Son*, a show that might as well have been a nature special with a laugh track, since, living as we did in a virtually all-white suburb, it provided our only exposure to people of color. As Fred Sanford feigned another heart attack, I nearly had one of my own. Mother appeared, canister vacuum and an eight-foot length of hose in hand.

"Hi, Billy," she said cheerily, as she made her way across the basement and began Hoovering off the pool table. "Don't mind me!"

Nothing was allowed to be left on the surface, including the balls, pool cues or chalk, but that hadn't stopped her from vacuuming it so many times that there were permanent brush marks in the green felt. Her cheerful demeanor scared me almost as much as the fact that she had surely noticed the pizza lying on the carpeting. At this moment, I couldn't be sure which was more dangerous.

She flipped off the vacuum and headed for the stairs. "Have a good time, you two!" she chirped, and disappeared upstairs.

Seconds later, an altogether different voice pierced the air from above.

"God in Heavennnn!!" she screamed at Dad. "If there are tomato sauce stains on that carpeting, you better start looking for a new family!"

Billy's eyes widened. "Is she all right?"

"Oh, fine, fine," I said airily, chuckling as though cries to the Holy Father were the most natural thing in the world. "She's rehearsing for a play." I glanced over casually to see if he had bought it. Fortunately, Billy was not always the brightest bulb in the chandelier.

"Ohhhhh," he replied, obviously relieved. "She's pretty good. Is she playing a crazy woman?"

I reached behind the faux-fur rocker to grab my coveted bedspread. "Oh, shoot, I forgot to have my mother throw this in the wash. Be right back."

I crossed into the laundry room, closing the door behind me, and knelt on the floor, burying my face in the bedspread as the high-volume shriekfest continued upstairs. "Dear Jesus," I began, "let the miracle of magic flow through me."

I visualized a calm descending over the house, a calm that kept Mother upstairs, quiet and hysteria-free, and a calm that allowed Billy to open his mind and heart so that the evil within could be purged. This night was proving to be more of a challenge than I had hoped, yet the moment of truth was coming. I knew it.

After a long and competitive game of Mousetrap, during which Mother mercifully calmed down and I silently thanked Jesus for his assistance with my magic, we turned on *The Midnight Special*, with host Little Richard and special guests Aerosmith and Kool and the Gang. Dad padded downstairs with a bag of potato chips, some snack cakes and another roll of paper towels. He surveyed the carpeting as he spread out a four-by-six-foot layer of paper towels.

"Your mother's gone to bed," he whispered. "Don't tell her I brought you this stuff or I'll wake up dead."

As Helen Reddy wailed "Delta Dawn," I casually snuck sidelong glances at Billy as he gorged on Ding Dongs. Bits of processed chocolate and chemical cream filling covered his face, yet even eating like a pig, he was handsome.

It was time.

As the fans screamed for "I Am Woman," I yawned loudly, stretching my arms, and rose to grab the two sleeping bags I had set in a corner. I unzipped them and spread one out on the floor.

"I'm beat."

I flipped off the TV, lay down on the pallet and pulled the other sleeping bag over me as a blanket. Billy surveyed the situation.

"Why don't we just each use a sleeping bag?"

"'Cause there's more room this way," I lied, certain that God would forgive me.

"Oh, gotcha." He climbed under the blanket. "It was a fun night."

I couldn't see his face. Was he staring at me admiringly, as I was him? My heart began to pound wildly. I had never cast out a demon before. Silently, I asked Jesus how this should best be accomplished. I took a deep breath, awaiting the answer, and within moments, it came.

As Billy's breathing began to become rhythmic, I stealthily inched closer to his body. Carefully, I lifted myself up and eased down on top of him. "Show him the way to Jesus," I prayed silently. My body was now fully engulfing his, my holy energy overpowering the demon within.

"Hey . . ." Billy awoke groggily. "What are you doing?"

"Jesus has sent me on a mission," I whispered. "Just go with it."

"Go with what?" he replied, annoyed. "You're heavy!"

Slowly, I began to rub my body against Billy's. "You have a demon," I said patiently. "It is my duty to squash it."

"I don't have any demon," Billy replied. "I'm an RA!"

The rubbing sensations felt surprisingly good. This is what it must feel like, I thought to myself, to be Jesus.

"Come on," Billy protested, now a little less vehemently, "knock it off."

There was a long pause. I continued to rub. "Really." His voice was softer now. A longer pause. "This . . . isn't . . . right."

He fell silent as the rubbing continued.

"I need to press harder," I whispered, my face near his although I couldn't see it. "I have to crush it. I have to crush the demon." My breathing was getting labored. Casting out evil was hard work, but worth it.

"But I don't have a de . . ." Billy's voice trailed off. I began to grind into him. A strange feeling began to fill my body, one I had never experienced. As it slowly began to build, an intensity of emotion and rapture I had never experienced began to overwhelm me.

"Dear Jesus," I wanted to scream, "help me fill him with your love!"

The feelings were washing over me like a tidal wave. I sensed the evil force within Billy getting ready to explode out of him.

Suddenly, he pushed me off with a violent shove. "Stop it!" He sat up and scooted away from me.

"But this is for your own good," I sputtered.

"It's weird!" He didn't sound entirely convinced. There was a moment of labored silence as we stared into the darkness. "*You're* weird!"

"I'm not *weird*!" I huffed. "I'm a good Baptist!"

"Then why do you want to do that to me?"

"This is for your own good. I'm casting out the—"

"You like it," he interrupted.

"Like what?"

"I don't know, touching me, or whatever. You like being with a boy, like the guy in that movie."

"No, I don't!"

He grabbed the sleeping bag blanket and folded it over into a single, crawling inside and turning his back to me. "I'm going to sleep."

"So am I!"

As we lay in standoff, my mind raced across an emotional landscape, from rage to denial to fear. I was doing my Christian duty. Wasn't I? I only wanted to save Billy from himself. Didn't I? Boys didn't need to beware of me.

Did they?

WE BARELY SPOKE in the morning. Although Dad had planned to take us to Dunkin' Donuts, Billy called his mom to pick him up first thing.

Trying to fill the uncomfortable silence that hung in the air, I grabbed my tennis shoes and began to tie the requisite plastic bags around them.

"C'mon, we can play Jarts!" I offered.

"What are you doing?" he said, as I secured the plastic bags with thick rubber bands.

"Oh, it's just easier," I explained. "This way I don't have to use the scrub brush and Bon Ami after."

He stared at me with an expression that bordered on disgust.

"No, thanks," he said flatly, looking down at his shoes as he kicked at imaginary dirt in the shag. "I'm just gonna wait outside." He walked out the front door and closed it quietly behind him.

Billy began to miss RA meetings.

And suddenly, even at Sunday school, he avoided me, speaking only when others were around. His behavior confused me. Anger I could deal with. Anger I could possibly counter. But he didn't seem angry; it was simply as though someone had flipped a switch inside him and he no longer cared.

But I cared. About the loss of my friend. About the strange feelings inside me. And about the question of how my magic—for so long now a real and potent part of my life—could have abandoned me when I needed it most. Was Jesus denying me the ability to create miracles? Or had he simply stopped listening?

NINE

Going with the Flo

My parents' best friends were the Edwardses, a couple they had met in the place where all true, rock-solid friendships are born: the Baptist Church. Only a couple of years older than Mother and Dad, they had three kids close in age to Val and me, and from the moment we moved to St. Louis, we socialized frequently. We attended church together, threw dinner parties for one another and, as with all long-time friendships, occasionally wished each other were dead.

Harvey and Florence "Flo" Edwards seemed to believe that their children could not only walk on water, but tap-dance on it as well. Flo, a cherubic housewife with a prematurely gray bouffant, was a thoughtful and generous woman who kept this notion to herself, but Harvey, her brilliant, intellectual husband, felt that this kind of information required wide and indiscriminate dissemination.

"What can I say," he would declare, leaning back in his dining room chair and nudging Dad after a recounting of his kids' most recent accomplishments, "when you're starting out with genes like mine . . ."

"Stop," Flo would admonish him, digging her nails into his forearm in an effort to rein him in. "I think it's high time we hear what Valerie and Eric have been up to."

This was usually the moment that stopped a dinner party cold. Ray and Elaine Poole had long since come to the conclusion that their children were far more likely to contract cancer than cure it. Although they relentlessly cheered Val and me on to the B grade averages they knew we had in us, our parents realized that when it came to bragging about their children, the Edwardses had it over them in spades.

Donny, their eldest child, was already, at age fifteen, a scientific genius who studied chemistry tables with all the fervor that I studied *TV Guide*. He was a tall, meticulous, dark-haired boy with thick Coke-bottle glasses, whose bookish personality lent the term "nerd" its rainbow of meaning.

Frances, their thirteen-year-old middle child, was

a brilliant and tortured actress. Wildly creative, she hadn't yet "grown into her looks" (as the adults around me explained it), resembling a teenage Miss Hathaway from *The Beverly Hillbillies*.

On the other hand, the youngest, Theresa, the most attractive of the three, seemed to come from somewhere else—perhaps the product of Flo's assignation with a hot but stupid repairman, given that she possessed few of the scientific or creative abilities of her siblings, and in fact found *It's the Great Pumpkin, Charlie Brown* frightening and difficult to follow. At age twelve, she was, to Val and me, the saving grace.

I actually enjoyed spending time with Frances, who was closest to my own age and with whom I could discuss such important issues as what the "stars" on *Tattletales* did the rest of the time, and why Jermaine was the Jackson brother to watch; but Mother and Dad pressed me to spend more time with both Frances *and* Donny, a duo that sent my self-esteem plummeting to spectacular new lows. The combination of Donny's analytical brilliance and Frances's creative genius seemed to leave no territory uncharted.

This was easily ignored when we were younger and the five of us spent the afternoon snorkeling in the Edwardses' plastic pool while Mrs. Edwards made us grilled cheese sandwiches and homemade pie. But now that Frances and I were in junior high, and Donny and Val were in high school, the gap between brilliance and stupefying ordinariness was, for Val and me, becoming all too clear.

In a desperate attempt to bridge the competitive gap, I took up the trumpet and, miraculously and quite out of nowhere, began to exhibit a fairly high level of skill. I immediately began to pound out the hit songs of the day with effusive energy and a complete lack of style. This newfound talent filled my sister with fear and loathing, since her inadequacies were now pointed out right in her own house. Yet we were both excited at the prospect of anything that would help level the playing field, since we were, at every turn, bested by the Edwards clan.

Perhaps the moment that crystallized our competition was when the Edwardses decided to enroll Donny and Frances in private schools. Not just parochial schools, which were the low-rent method of privatizing a child's education, but prestigious prep schools that routinely sent their graduates on to the finest Ivy League institutions.

The announcement came over dinner at our house.

"The public school system is a shambles," Harvey announced, evidently forgetting that his less exceptional daughter was still enrolled in it. "And the best thing you can do for gifted progeny is give them the proper tools to excel," he declared, as he gazed lovingly at two of his three kids.

"Of course, we're proud of all our children," Flo

chimed in, in an attempt to include Theresa, who was busy staring at a tin bas-relief on the wall, certain that John the Baptist's eyes were following her. Flo motioned to Val and me. "Just like you're proud of these two wonderful kids."

"Yeah, long as they don't end up in jail," Dad replied as he winked at us. Mother kicked him under the table so hard that his eyes began to water.

For reasons that completely eluded Val and me, Mother could be not only friendly but downright delightful to people she liked, and her friendship with Flo was long-standing and supportive. Her feelings about Harvey, however, were slightly less congenial, and Mother, although rarely complimentary to our faces, was not about to take Harvey's arrogance lying down.

"Well, I think Valerie and Eric are doing just *fine* in public school."

"True," Harvey replied. "That Eric's turning into quite the trumpet player. I'll bet one day he might even make first chair, like Donny did last year with the trombone." Harvey paused to offer me the sympathetic smile of the truly superior. We waited for him to compliment Val, but he had obviously reached his quota.

"Yeah," he continued, "we're enrolling them this fall. I think private school will really send the right message." He turned to Donny and Frances. "My kids want to be more than just big fish in a small pond, don't you?" Donny and Frances nodded with Pavlovian enthusiasm.

"I don't know where he gets off," Mother declared a couple hours later, as she slammed open the velvet-lined flatware case and replaced the silver forks, which, although only two years old, had been polished down to their core metal. "Flo is a doll, but Harvey just *lives* to lord those kids over us."

"Oh, he doesn't mean anything by it," Dad said loudly, as he flipped on the Hoover canister to vacuum the kitchen carpeting.

"Are you kidding?" Mother shouted. "Any day now I fully expect one of those kids to turn water into wine. And Harvey will serve it to us as the Blood of Donny."

LATE THAT NIGHT, I sat alone in my faux-fur rocking chair in the basement (a perhaps not surprisingly discontinued design from Mother's employer), fingering the old chenille bedspread that had served as my connection to the mystical realms.

I no longer envisioned my magical ability as supernatural, of course, since I had learned that the power emanated from God. And in fact, I was no longer convinced that I still possessed any such power, since God's granting of my magical requests had become sporadic and devoid of reason. Yet whether out of habit or some perverse hope, I persisted, closing my eyes and attempting to inhale the power of this once-mighty costume, desperate to prove that with his help, I could still change the course of events.

As I buried my face in the dusty fabric, I closed my eyes and began to listen intently. Slowly, in the distance, I could hear the roar of people cheering. Gradually, the sound became closer, and louder, enveloping everything around me. Thousands of people were stomping their feet and screaming applause. I felt the heat of lighters as I magically floated through the darkness into an arena. I settled on a stage before a crowd of fifteen thousand, holding my trumpet and taking bows with the superstar band Chicago.

I peered past the footlights to see the Edwards family in the front row. They formed a sliding scale of approval, from Flo, Frances and Theresa's wild cheering to Donny's restrained clapping to Harvey's stone face. I grabbed one of the heavy metal mouthpieces for my trumpet and tossed it to Frances as a souvenir. My aim was bad and she didn't see it, and when it slammed into her head and she began to bleed from a large gash, Harvey rounded up the family and stomped out. Fans dove for the mouthpiece, scratching and clawing one another in a desperate attempt to snatch a piece of history.

A woman held up the slightly red-stained mouthpiece

with a broad smile. I gave her a thumbs-up and the crowd went wild.

GIVEN THE now tenuous nature of my connection to magic, I had little confidence that this request would be granted. So it was with shock and elation that I greeted my promotion from third to second chair in band class that fall. God seemed to be listening once again! Why he had chosen to grant this request and not others remained a mystery, but somehow, my magical connection had been at least momentarily restored.

With his help, my talents as a trumpeter began to skyrocket; and no one took more note of this than Mother, who viewed this accomplishment as ammunition for the next Edwards dinner party.

Harvey, however, apparently foresaw this turn of events and decided to kick things up a notch. Over buttermilk fried chicken and mashed potatoes at the Edwards home, he announced their latest first.

Donny, having mastered the scientific frontier, had now ventured into the creative realms and written a play. His professors at the snotty Chadwick School were, according to Harvey, practically wetting themselves.

"The director wants to produce it as is," Donny noted, glancing at his father, who was practically mouthing the words along with him, "but I feel like I should at least attempt a rewrite. I mean, I only did the one draft. It just doesn't seem like it should be this easy."

I had some conjuring to do.

OVER THE NEXT FEW MONTHS, I redoubled my basement efforts at both music and magic. Val was routinely annoyed by my loud and emotionally over-wrought renditions of "Time in a Bottle" and "Touch Me in the Morning"; she nonetheless cheered me on, since we both realized that my musical ability rep-resented our only real hope of deliverance from the oppression of Harvey Edwards.

My musical improvement was complicated by the arrival of braces on my teeth, which made it painfully difficult to play, since the sharp metal tore open the inner tissue of my lips with such regularity that I kept a large wad of tissue in my jeans to sop up the blood.

But I could not and would not be distracted from my goal, and finally, that spring, having won the admiration of the band director, I was rewarded with a promotion to first chair.

This extraordinary (for the Pooles) accomplishment was debuted at a church potluck when the Edwards kids were absent, chosen specifically by Mother for its larger audience and potential for Harvey humiliation.

"I don't know where he gets his musical talent," Mother declared in as modest a tone as she could muster under these extraordinary circumstances, as she signaled me to open my trumpet case.

"Yeah," Dad added before Mother could take aim at his perpetually bandaged shin, "it's not like prodigies are falling off *our* family tree."

Flo turned to me and clapped her hands. "Play something for us."

Surprisingly willing to display my only marketable talent, and thrilled to have the attention of adults for any reason other than pity, I let loose with a swinging rendition of "Rock of Ages," to the considerable horror of our pastor, who stopped me midway through and asked that I never play a hymn that way again. God was apparently aghast, but the crowd clapped appreciatively, especially Flo.

Harvey dutifully joined in the applause, then paused a moment before leaning forward to my parents to bark, "Guess what?"

"What's that?" Mother replied as she took a sip of coffee, still basking in this rare moment of glory. I wondered if she would actually stand and curtsy.

"Donny's gonna graduate early! An entire year early, can you believe that?" His voice boomed as he turned to acknowledge the looks of wild admiration from those around us.

Mother nearly choked on her Taster's Choice as

Dad shot her a pleading "Don't say anything" look. Parents at nearby tables smiled the teeth-baring sneer of the freshly one-upped. Harvey acknowledged their jealousy with a tastefully modest "Smell me!" grin.

"Oh, it's nothing," Flo interjected quietly, smiling at Val and me. "I'm sure Eric and Valerie could do it, too. I just worry about a boy his age being in college."

"Nothing?" Harvey replied. "My son is gonna be the first sixteen-year-old from St. Louis in the Ivy League!"

We had no idea where he had come up with this college statistic—surely a city with a million-plus population had, over the course of the past century, produced one genius who had managed to get sprung from high school early. But without hard facts, we couldn't dispute him.

"Well, isn't that wonderful," Mother said as she lifted her coffee cup and smiled. "And how's Theresa?"

I SAT ALONE in the basement with my bedspread. Fresh out of other talents, I knew that only drastic action could save my parents from permanent humiliation. I feared that if Val and I didn't come up with an alternative soon, Mother and Dad would have to quit our church in disgrace. We would be forever branded losers, forced to wear scarlet *L*'s and suffer the scorn of four-fifths of the Edwards clan for all time.

Silently, I asked God for something to even the score. Something simple. Something unique.

OVER THE NEXT YEAR, Frances and I began to discover that we had more and more in common and began to spend a lot of time together, always at the Edwardses' home. Although our love for the arts was one of the interests that bonded Frances and me, the theatrical rages that Mother performed nightly were not the type of performances I felt would inform Frances's craft.

Donny, although frequently at home, was busy attempting nuclear fission in the basement and couldn't be bothered with IQs under 200. Theresa could usually be found rehearsing the *Gilligan's Island* theme song in the den, and after several hundred reruns, was tantalizingly close to memorizing it.

Mrs. Edwards, on the other hand, enjoyed being on hand for the shows we regularly premiered in their living room. I played sensitive, muted trumpet as underscore to Frances's interpretive readings from the likes of Sylvia Plath and Rizzo from *Grease*. We frequently had no idea what they meant, but we both scowled a lot to indicate the vast pools of emotional depth we were plumbing.

Always an enthusiastic supporter, Mrs. Edwards seemed to grow increasingly moved by these performances as our shows began to reflect ever more insightful (to us) observations of the human condition. As the months passed, she often began to look stricken halfway through the show, and by the finale would clap quietly, and then disappear into the bedroom, obviously to contemplate the profundity of what she had just seen.

My appreciation of her support, along with the fact that the year had passed relatively competition-free, had begun to change the dynamic between our families. Harvey, in particular, seemed to mellow a bit, his traditionally overbearing style replaced with a quieter demeanor that verged on pleasant. This pronounced change of character alternately confused and thrilled Val and me. Had we finally achieved a level of respect in Harvey's eyes?

The answer seemed to come over dinner at our house, when Harvey premiered his kids' latest achievements. Mrs. Edwards had stayed home with the flu, so when he quieted us all to make his latest announcement, we assumed it would come with a heaping helping of braggadocio.

"I guess I always hoped Donny would make the Ivy League," Harvey began, suddenly sliding into a level of personal reflection we were highly unaccustomed to. "Make up for the fact that I went to such a crappy school." I caught a quick glance between Mother and Dad, who were obviously surprised by this admission as well. "He got accepted to MIT."

Val and I had no idea what MIT was or where it was located, but it sounded impressive and obviously was.

Normally, during an announcement this big, Harvey would be soaking up the attention like a pharaoh receiving his supplicants. But he just sat there, moving the peas around his plate and smiling an odd, distant smile as we all turned to congratulate Donny.

MRS. EDWARDS MISSED church three weeks in a row.

"What's up with your mom?" I whispered to Frances as we sat together in the back pew.

"Her flu turned into pneumonia," Frances replied.

"Yikes! Isn't pneumonia something old people get?"

"Yeah. But she's forty-two, that's pretty old."

That night, as we drove to church for round two of Sunday services, I dug for more information.

"What's pneumonia?"

"Pneumonia?" Dad asked. "It's a respiratory infection. Like a bad cold in your lungs. Remember, Grandma Ruth had it." I didn't remember. "Why?" he asked.

" 'Cause Mrs. Edwards has it."

I saw Mother, who always rode with the passenger-side visor down (so she could evaluate herself in the vanity mirror that was clipped to it) shoot a glance at Dad. There was silence.

"How long before she's better?" I asked.

More silence. I stared at Mother and Dad. Why was no one speaking?

"She doesn't have pneumonia," Mother said without turning around. "She has cancer."

I felt as though I'd had the wind knocked out of me. CANCER. That was bad. People die from cancer.

"Is she gonna be all right?"

Another long pause. "We don't know." I stared at the visor mirror. Mother appeared to have tears in her eyes. She glanced back with the sudden realization that she was being watched, and flipped the visor up with a snap.

The Edwards clan was absent from church that night. I called Frances the minute we returned home.

"Your mom doesn't have pneumonia, does she?"

"No," Frances responded quietly. "But Dad doesn't want us to tell people." I heard her voice catch.

My mind reeled. What had I done? I had invoked my magical abilities to even the score, completely unaware of the potential consequences. Had I somehow brought this upon her?

Since my mother was closest to the situation, I decided she would have the most insight, painful as it would likely be to extract. Later that night, as she was ironing place mats in the laundry room, I crept in, fumbling with the doorknob so as to indicate my approach, since her sotto voce mumblings, a popular feature of her laundry room stints, included thoughts and opinions about my father, our relatives and her job that were not exactly candy to a young boy's ears.

"I wish he were *dead*," Mother muttered, shooting steam onto the place mat as though she held a handgun.

I cleared my throat as further indication that another, potentially impressionable human was present.

"One day, as God is my witness, I'm gonna poison that idiot."

"Just came to get a magazine," I said by way of apology as I began rifling through the stack of *Mad* magazines in my toy chest, hoping that she was referring to one of the mice that periodically took up residence in our basement.

"Did I hear the water in the kitchen?" she barked.

"No, uh-uh, it was the bathroom," I replied quickly, knowing that had I gotten the kitchen sink wet, all bets were off.

"Well, hurry up."

I pulled out one magazine, then another, sizing up the contents intently. Another shot of steam *psss*ed forth from the iron as Mother set her jaw, intent on making those wrinkles relent.

"That's really sad," I began, peering intently at

the cover of *Mad* issue #802. I waited for a response. None came. "About Mrs. Edwards."

More steam. "It's a tragedy," Mother replied.

"She'll get better, right?" I said hopefully.

Mother didn't look up. "It doesn't look good. It's spread to her lymph nodes."

I didn't know what lymph nodes were, but they sounded ominous. "How come she has cancer?" I asked in as offhand a voice as I could muster. "Did she get exposed to radiation or something?"

"Who knows? Why does anyone get cancer?" Mother replied. "It just happens. It's God's will."

"Why?"

Mother sighed heavily. "Ask your father."

Dad was upstairs in his corduroy La-Z-Boy, nodding off to *Starsky & Hutch*. I tapped his arm with the *Mad* magazine.

"It wasn't on the list!" he mumbled defensively.

"Dad?"

His eyes opened. "What's wrong?"

"Mother said to ask you why Mrs. Edwards has cancer."

He shook himself awake and handed me a Slim Jim from his secret stash behind the fireplace tools. "Nobody knows," he replied gently. "There are just some things we're not meant to understand. It's just a part of God's plan."

"But what if—"

"Eric, you can't 'what if.' God knows better than we do."

THE MONTHS DRAGGED ON, and as Mrs. Edwards slowly got worse, so did my panic. She had been in and out of the hospital five times. She had lost nearly sixty pounds and was confined to bed as the chemotherapy stripped her body not only of the cancer cells, but of all healthy ones as well.

Every afternoon now, I planted myself in the basement rocker and buried my face in the bedspread. I summoned all my powers to envision Mrs. Edwards rising out of her bed, plump and cherubic once again, to make raspberry pie and applaud our performance of the climactic scene from that week's episode of *Good Times*.

For brief moments, it would appear to be working; Flo would attend church, weak but present, a brunette bouffant wig gracing her now bald head. Then word would come of a relapse. She would be back in the hospital. The cancer had spread yet again.

The final blow came when it infected her bones. Her body was now so ravaged that any hope of a miracle had long since been abandoned. Mother, Val, Dad and I stood with Harvey in the vestibule of our church as friends stopped to offer words of support and encouragement. Harvey just nodded, unable to respond.

As the last of the parishioners departed, he turned to Mother and Dad, quietly choking back tears. His expression said it all, and without a word, they each put a hand on his shoulder.

He glanced into their eyes and then quickly looked away, afraid that their expressions might open a floodgate in him. "I think this may be it."

DAD AND I were grilling Spam on the barbecue for lunch. I turned to him.

"Are you guys gonna go see Mrs. Edwards again?"

"Yeah, probably tonight."

"Can I go?"

Throughout Mrs. Edwards's hospital stays, I had been too afraid to visit her, always begging off, and Mother and Dad had never pressed the issue. But I knew that if I was ever to confess my role in what had happened to her, it had to be now.

"Sure," Dad replied. "But you can't talk too much. She's pretty sick."

That evening, we made the trek to Barnes, a noted cancer hospital in the city. As a suburban kid, I should have been marveling at the exotic urban blight as we drove through the depressed downtown area of St. Louis—look, bullet holes! Wow, a body in a Dumpster!—but I was busy envisioning a dramatic healing that I knew in my heart I didn't have the power to pull off.

When we arrived, Harvey ushered us into the room. Mrs. Edwards smiled feebly as we entered. The vibrant woman I knew was gone. She was gaunt, and her thin, papery skin had a yellowish color. She seemed to have aged fifty years.

Mother made a slight whimpering sound, shocked at the change since her last visit. She rounded the bed and immediately took Flo's hand. Flo said simply, "Elaine," as if it were a precious, sacred word, and in that moment I realized the bond between the two women. Mother blinked back tears as she raised Flo's hand to her face, then lightly kissed her fingers, one by one, a gesture of such warmth and intimacy that it shocked me.

I stood watching them as they whispered together, until an African-American nurse entered. Her name tag read Loretta.

"Can y'all give us a minute?" she said to the assembled group.

"We'll be right back," Mother said to Flo as she gently laid her hand on the bed and stepped away, allowing Loretta access. Harvey opened the door and ushered Mother and Dad out, closing it behind him, obviously forgetting I was present. The nurse made a move to shoo me out, but Flo whispered, "Let him stay."

I crossed to the opposite side of the bed as the nurse changed a hanging plastic bag.

"It was very sweet of you to come," Flo said haltingly, every word obviously an effort. "I've missed you."

"I'm so sorry!" I blurted out.

The corners of her mouth turned up in a faint smile. "Me too. You're gonna be somebody. I wanted to be there to see it."

"No," I stopped her. "I'm sorry for—"

She suddenly gasped. "Oh, look!" She raised her arm slightly and pointed to the foot of her bed. "Daddy's here."

There was no man in the room. I glanced at the nurse, unsure what to make of this.

Without missing a beat, Loretta leaned down to whisper into Flo's ear. "He's here to take you to the Promised Land," she said quietly. "There's nothing to be afraid of."

"Oh, I'm not afraid," Flo replied. She stared across the room, smiling for a long moment at nothing. Finally, Loretta patted Flo's hand and opened the door for the others to return.

On the way home from the hospital, I related to Mother and Dad what had transpired while they were out of the room.

Mother clucked her tongue sadly. "Her father's

been dead for almost ten years. She's hallucinating now. It must be the drugs."

Dad nodded. "But at least she's not in pain."

THE CALL CAME a few nights later as Dad and I were watching *Kojak*. Mother never answered the phone, always expecting us to tell people that she was "out"—although where she would be at this hour on a weeknight was anyone's guess. Helping the insomniac poor?

Dad went to their bedroom to answer the phone. There was a pause, and then he shuffled back down the hall to the laundry chute, our intercom to Mother's basement lair.

"Elaine?" he yelled into it.

Mother trudged up the stairs silently. As she passed by us, I stared at the TV, not wanting to lock eyes with her. Dad followed her quietly into the bedroom, closing the door behind them.

"SHE'S IN a better place now."

I had heard this line before when people passed away—but I wondered if Mrs. Edwards was *supposed* to be in Heaven. Maybe she was supposed to be alive for Frances's triumph on Broadway. Or Donny's invention of the flying car. Or Theresa's recitation of the ingredients of a Big Mac. Maybe she was supposed to see me play the trumpet at Carnegie Hall.

How could God have allowed this? I had invoked magic to compete with the Edwardses. But this was not how I wanted to win the game.

MR. EDWARDS seemed changed. It was as though the light had gone out in his eyes. After a time, we began to have the family over to dinner again. But the palpable emptiness in the room and in his smile was a source of pain so potent that, whether through kindness or cowardice, Mother and Dad elected to give the situation some time to heal.

But nothing could heal the growing fear inside me. Whether I regarded this tragedy as the darkest possible interpretation of a magical request, or simply the random act of an angry and vengeful creator, it seemed frighteningly clear that the God I once knew had indeed left the building.

TEN

What a Friend
We Have *in Jesus

I had always considered myself a compassionate figure, a benevolent soul in the spirit of Martin Luther King, Jr., Marcus Welby, M.D., or Big Bird. As someone with such munificent qualities, I naturally abhorred violence of any kind, particularly that rendered upon small animals or seventh-graders.

Thus, it was with great distress that I greeted the revelation that Albert Anderson, one of the neighbor kids, had a thing for torturing defenseless creatures.

My discovery that he had graduated from setting ants on fire with a magnifying glass came one afternoon as I was sitting on the patio enjoying some delicious Kraft macaroni and cheese. Out of the corner of my eye I saw a flash of red hair and freckles. Albert shot past our backyard.

A strip of common ground ran behind all the properties on our side of the street, thus making it easy for nosy neighbors to scope out what was happening in your yard at pretty much any given time. Likewise, since few of us had privacy fences, there was no missing the activity that occurred on the common ground.

I glanced up to see that Albert (whom I referred to as Fat Albert to anyone who was unlikely to repeat it to him) was carrying a BB gun—a weapon that was, at best, ill advised for someone with a flair for persecution. He stopped in his tracks and raised the gun.

"Hey, Albert!" I hollered in my friendliest voice. Albert was, obviously, a lot wider than me, and although he had never really threatened me, I figured it wise to hedge my bets.

He ignored me and took aim at something. *Ping!*

I jumped up. "Hey, whatcha doin'?"

"Tryin' to nab me a squirrel."

"For what?" I replied, agitated. "Some Jed Clampett stew?"

Albert pumped the gun and raised it again. I saw a small brown squirrel scampering slowly up the trunk of a tree, his head cocked nervously as if aware that danger was near, but not quite sure from where.

Ping!

"Albert!" I screamed, trying to divert his attention

so the poor little nut scavenger could make a getaway. Val and I had owned pet guinea pigs since shortly after our arrival in St. Louis, and it felt as though Albert were taking aim at one of their cousins.

Albert paid no attention. He shot again. "Gotcha!"

He rushed over to collect his wounded trophy, but the panicked squirrel managed to limp to freedom through the chain-link fence of the high school.

I hurried out toward the common ground, staying just inside the perimeter of our yard in case events took a turn for the worse.

"Why do you wanna shoot things that can't shoot back?" I said in as unchallenging a tone as possible. "Not much of a competition, is it?"

"He deserves it." Albert's Wrangler Huskies were riding low, and I could see his big white butt-crack, which threatened to reverse the gravitational voyage of my macaroni and cheese.

"Why? He didn't do anything to you."

"He was in my yard."

"So was the Mulligans' dog, but you didn't shoot him." I immediately regretted this statement. Albert didn't have much going on in that fat head of his, so there was plenty of room for the planting of an idea.

"Yeah, well, you can't kill a dog that big with a BB gun." He obviously *had* put some thought into it. He turned and marched off in search of another woodland creature.

. . .

I TOLD Darren Pulaski about Albert.

Darren was an older and wiser Royal Ambassador from church whose criminal tendencies gave him an exotic edge. He had been known to steal Ding Dongs from the Quick Shop—slipping the cellophane-wrapped cakes between his buttocks, which, to me, seemed unnecessarily complicated—and had once been "almost arrested" (according to him) for a crime he was not at liberty to discuss.

We were strictly church friends—he wanted nothing to do with me outside of that venue—but there Darren imparted the many insights he had gleaned from nearly twelve extra months of living, as we walked up and down the darkened hallway of an unused section of the church that he regularly broke into just to prove that he could.

"It's just a squirrel," Darren said, mystified.

He pulled a cigarette out of his pocket and nonchalantly stuck it in his mouth without lighting it. He pretended to smoke, inhaling loudly and exhaling through pursed lips, a look of utter cool pasted across his face. "If Albert didn't kill it, a bear probably would."

Given Darren's status as an elder, I hesitated to point out that there weren't a lot of grizzlies roaming around the Wedgwood Green subdivision.

"But the bear would eat it, right? Albert was just trying to kill it for fun."

"Yeah, that part kinda stinks," he said, flicking a nonexistent ash off the cigarette. "But there's a lot of stuff in the world that doesn't make any sense. You just gotta roll with it."

ALTHOUGH I CONSIDERED myself to possess many illustrious talents, Rolling With It was not even on the list. Sitting in the basement with the once mighty bedspread on my lap, I closed my eyes.

"We *have to* stop him," I demanded to a God I wasn't at all sure was listening.

I had always believed that my magic could triumph over evil. But given the events of the past couple of years, this was seeming less and less likely to hold true. But surely, I thought, God wouldn't doom little animals to the same kind of treatment he imposed on his human children. Surely he would heed a magical request for creatures so powerless.

I began to visualize the common ground behind our house suddenly filled with squirrels, rabbits and moles—a glorious, enchanted meadow where these guileless creatures romped and played, unwary of human interlocutors. Albert appeared, gun in hand, and, without concern for their safety, the animals jumped on him, licking his face, sliding merrily down the barrel of his weapon, the squirrels begging him to be their companion. He dropped his gun and, overcome by their pure, innocent joy, joined them in a game of nut relay.

I HAD NOT SEEN Albert in more than a week, and God had, in my eyes, begun to redeem himself. It was reassuring to feel that he understood the needs of the meek; that perhaps he did, after all, hold the most downtrodden in his big, heavenly hands.

I once again started to enjoy relaxing on the patio, reading and listening to KSLQ while trying to be the ninety-eighth caller.

Then, one afternoon as I sat reading a compendium of the finest literary pieces from *Cracked* magazine, I heard the dreaded *ping*.

Albert ran past, whooping. He stopped on the common ground and picked up a small animal. From a hundred feet away, it looked like a rabbit. It seemed to be squirming, as if it had been hurt but was still alive.

I was aghast. Albert set the animal back on the ground, and it began to limp away. Well, at least, I thought, he's gonna let it go lick its wounds. God had stopped him from doing something truly heinous. Maybe it's not that big a deal if he just hurts 'em a little. They'll heal. I've gotten lots of bruises and scratches and I'm none the worse for wear.

I watched as Albert stood over the animal, apparently making sure that it could walk and would be okay. Then he lifted his leg over it.

What is he doing? I wondered. I stood up to get a better look—just in time to see him *stomp* on its head. He paused, and stomped again.

My mouth fell open. Apparently satisfied that he had killed the creature, Albert picked up his gun and marched off without a sound, a look of smug satisfaction on his face.

I stood frozen in place on the patio. As Albert headed toward the creek and disappeared from view, I finally dropped my book and slipped across the backyard to the common ground.

A small, gray rabbit lay there, bleeding, its eyes closed.

I watched it for signs of life. It wasn't breathing.

I touched it. It felt dead.

My blood began to boil. This poor little guy had done nothing to him, and he had killed it. I wanted to run after Albert, to grab that gun and smash it down on his head so hard that his skull split open in front of me. I wanted to watch him bleed, see *him* die.

WHAT A FRIEND *we have in Jesus* . . .

These ironic words were sung by me, Mother, Dad and the two hundred other sweaty congregants of Florissant Valley Baptist Church. Sunday morning was unconscionably warm and humid, and I was melting under my plaid sport jacket and clip-on tie, wondering just how much praise I had to give this Supremely Indifferent Being before he'd let me go home and put on shorts.

All our sins and griefs to bear . . .

Exactly whose grief was he bearing? I wondered, as I held the heavy blue hymnal. Certainly not mine, or the rabbit's. I sang dutifully in the official Baptist singing style, a dirgelike voice that made every song sound like we were about to put a bullet in our heads. I had once asked Dad why we didn't sing like those black audiences on televangelist shows, and he explained that that kind of carrying on made God mad.

What a privilege to carry everything to God in prayer.

Maybe for you guys, I thought, gazing down the pew at the Reynolds family, and the Clarksons. Mr. Clarkson was slumped over, snoring. Mrs. Clarkson used to elbow him, but after he had told her a few weeks back to "leave me alone or I'll be tithing ten percent of your booze fund," she just let him be.

Although I'd never really paid any attention to the hymns we sang like soldiers on a death march, today the lyrics struck me as completely absurd. Jesus was not my friend.

Once we had finished (the Almighty required all

hosannahs to be sung standing, which made me wonder about the hereafter prospects for Dave Wornack, a recent Vietnam vet who was in a wheelchair), we sat back down.

"Our Lord God," Pastor Thompson said, his voice booming from the pulpit, "is always with us. Through joy and through sorrow, he is at our side."

Outside of his dire warnings about the consequences of wrongdoing (Romans 6:23, "The wages of sin is death"), I'd never really bothered to contemplate what the pastor said. His sermons were eternally long, and I generally passed the time singing Tony Orlando and Dawn songs in my head and wondering if there was a biblically mandated amount of worship time (since we also attended services on Sunday and Wednesday nights), or if those extra services were just an insurance policy, a sort of Allstate plan for the afterlife.

I had taken Jesus Christ as my personal savior when I was seven years old, shortly before we left Cedar Rapids, Iowa, and had, at the time, assumed I had done everything necessary to earn an Express ticket to Heaven, bypassing the Pearly Gates as I was ushered through the celebrity VIP entrance. I had, after all, allowed the pastor to shove me underwater during a Sunday morning service, no small sacrifice given that baptism completely wrecked my hair.

But it seemed clear now that God was not at my side. Maybe he had never been with me at all.

"Who among us," Pastor Thompson boomed, "has not endured the pain of a loved one's death? Many have walked through that dark valley."

Mr. Clarkson snored at the other end of the pew. I used my hymnal as a fan as I hung, for one of the first times ever, on the pastor's every word.

"But Christ's resurrection," he bellowed, "conquers all. Though death follows us closely in this life, it will be banished in the next."

Did this apply to rabbits? I wondered. Was that little gray rabbit bounding around in Heaven with Mrs. Edwards and, hopefully, those people from the bus accident? Did a rabbit have to get "right with God"?

As the Sunday morning service ended and Mother and Dad chatted with friends, I stole up to the front of the church.

"Pastor Thompson?" I called from a few feet away, standing off to one side.

He excused himself from the couple he was chatting with and crossed over to me. Although he reminded me of Dad, his tall stature, gray hair and solemn preaching style gave him a sterner edge and made me frequently envision him standing at the Pearly Gates with a clipboard, advising congregants that—for reasons they knew all too well—their names were not on the guest list.

"Hello, Eric," he said in his most magisterial tone. "What can I do for you today?"

I leaned in, as if to shush him. "Can I ask you a question?" I whispered.

"Sure," he whispered back, a note of bemusement in his voice.

"Do animals go to Heaven?"

He put his hand on my shoulder. "Oh, I'm sorry. Did you just lose a pet?"

"Sort of," I replied uncomfortably. I didn't want to get into specifics, since he'd probably think I was crazy. It was just a wild rabbit.

"We don't know for sure," he said kindly. "There's no real proof that pets have souls."

"But people do, right?"

"Well, of course."

"So animals just die and that's it?"

"Well, they provide lots of love to us human beings and we do the same for them, so their lives are not in vain."

"But what if they die before their time? Do they get another shot?"

"Eric," he said kindly, "there's no such thing as reincarnation. Animals are a gift to the world, but you can't worry about their journey. Everything will be explained when we get to Heaven."

Boy, I thought to myself, when I arrive in Paradise, God's sure got a lot of splainin' to do. Pastor Thompson gazed at me to see if his words had had their intended effect. I smiled wanly and thanked him as he patted my shoulder and walked off.

"HE SOUNDS LIKE A PSYCHO," Darren said that night, when I told him of Albert's brutal killing of the rabbit. "I'd stay away from that creep, or you might be next."

He pulled a slightly crumpled cigarette out of his shirt pocket. "But I'll come visit your grave if he kills you. I'll sit on your tombstone and smoke."

"Isn't it wrong to just kill things for fun?" I asked as we paced the darkened hallway of the church.

"Well, I wouldn't kill a *person*. You could go to the slammer for that."

"But it's okay to kill an animal?"

"You can't sweat the small stuff."

"But that's not small! That rabbit probably had a family and maybe some friends, and—"

"I figure," Darren replied with authority, "if it ain't hurting another *person*—you know, like a human being—it's small stuff. I mean, I cheat in school all the time. That's not hurting anybody."

"Hmmm," I said, politely brushing aside my curiosity at how it was possible for him to cheat all the time and still be flunking eighth grade. "But don't you ever worry," I said hesitantly, "that God'll get you in the end?"

"Nah," he said. "I'm not sure if I believe in all this God stuff."

This was the first time I had ever heard someone say this aloud. The only atheist I had ever seen was that woman Madalyn Murray O'Hair, who was on the news because she sued to end prayer in schools, and Mother and Dad had assured me that she was a sad and lonely woman who would one day be rotating on a spit in Hell.

It was blasphemous to think such a thing. Wasn't it?

As we strode up and down the darkened hallway in silence, I slowly began to replay the "magical" moments of my past.

What if Dad had not returned to the family after his fight with Mother years ago through any mystical ministrations of mine? I wondered. What if he had returned merely from a sense of duty, or obligation?

What if I had not magically won the friendship of Stacy, my armless fourth-grade classmate? What if, since we were both outcasts, it was simply convenient, or inevitable?

What if Mother's confrontation with Grandma Dorothy had not been created as a moment of understanding for me, but was simply a long-brewing dispute destined to explode?

And what if the events with a bus, a Royal Ambassador, cancer and now Albert were the natural outcomes of a world where God, if he even exists, has better things to do?

These moments of "magic," events that I thought had given me both a mystical connection to God and some measure of control over my world, suddenly seemed like nothing more than twists of fate. And as we drove home from church that night, and I sat silently in the backseat staring out the window at the stars, the truth slowly began to settle down upon me like a thick, suffocating blanket.

Magic doesn't exist.

We're all on our own.

I HAD PUT the rabbit in a Kinney shoe box and hidden it behind the shrubs on the side of the house, waiting for the appropriate moment when no one was home to give him a proper burial. I knew that Dad would have helped me, but in case I got choked up, I didn't want him to see me cry.

It was Monday afternoon, and Mother and Dad were at work. Val was in her bedroom with the door closed, whispering into the telephone like an informant for the mob.

The box was starting to smell funny. A weird, sickly sweet odor permeated the bushes as I pulled it out, and I nearly vomited up the box of Ding Dongs I had just eaten (having found them inside the basement ceiling, one of the secret locations where Mother hid snacks so we wouldn't gorge on them all at once).

I couldn't bear to open the box. I solemnly carried it to a spot just outside the perimeter of our lawn, shaded somewhat by one of the fruit trees that bordered the yard. I glanced right and left to be sure that no one was watching, and, with a hand shovel, began to dig into the matted brown grass of the common ground.

"I bless you," I said silently to this forsaken little animal, trying not to blow chunks as the malodorous stench hung in the lifeless air. "I bless you."

When enough earth had been displaced, I carefully set the shoe box into the hole. I covered the box with dirt, taking care to pack it tightly and pat the top layer of soil smooth so that no one would be the wiser. I briefly considered crafting a small grave marker to memorialize this Tomb of the Unknown Soldier, but thought better of this, since Albert might see it and exhume him so he could fry him up.

"I'm sorry I couldn't save you," I whispered. "I'm not the witch I thought I was."

THE NEXT EVENING, as Mother was eliminating clutter by assembling a bag of donations for the Disabled Veterans (a charity she generously supported by giving away anything that wasn't nailed down),

I slipped down to the basement and pulled out my old bedspread.

The cloth was usually a bit musty, crammed as it always was behind the chair. But tonight, I noticed that it seemed to be lint-free and smelled of fabric softener. That's odd, I thought. If Mother had come across it, she wouldn't have returned it to this hiding place—would she? I sniffed it again. It must just be my imagination.

I fingered the worn white fabric. Those days of childish belief in magic seemed as distant as my friend-ship with an armless girl. It was time, I thought, to let go of a past that was nothing more than a fantasy.

I carried the bedspread upstairs and, when Mother was out of the room, began to remove the top layer of clothing from the donation bag in order to slip the blanket underneath. I wanted no questions about from whence this item had come. As I gently placed it in the bag, I began to recall the hundreds of after-noons that this worn, pilled piece of material had been my comfort, my confidant, my connection to a mystical realm.

Then I reached to snatch it back from the pile. It wasn't as if I still believed that throwing a bedspread over my shoulders could change my life. But it had been an important part of my history, and it seemed disrespectful, somehow, to simply send it off to some guy with no hands.

But I stopped myself. Because I knew in my heart the truth: it was time to move on.

"CAN I get a BB gun?"

Dad and I were lying in the family room watching a *Land of the Giants* rerun. For some time I had been saving my allowance for a fringed suede jacket, but suddenly, thanks to Albert, the idea of gun ownership now seemed more appealing.

Dad had always patiently attempted to interest me in traditional male pursuits like vegetable gardening and home improvements, hobbies of his that I found tolerable only as long as he let me recap *Here's Lucy* episodes throughout. And fortunately, he had never forced me to take up sports. Yet he was strangely delighted at my interest in shooting.

"Sure, you can get one. But you have to be very careful with it. You can blow off a guy's grape nuts with a gun like that."

Val was now working part-time at Kmart, and several days later she furtively called Dad from the store.

"Red Ryder Blue Light," she whispered into the phone, in code. "Hurry."

Dad and I hightailed it up to Kmart in time to purchase the popular Daisy Red Ryder BB gun at the Blue Light Special price of just $12.99. Screaming kids surrounded the whirling blue light, pulling the guns out of their boxes and aiming them at frightened passersby as the manager rushed up and informed the crowd that "anyone who shoots a customer will be arrested!"—conveniently leaving the employees out of the equation as several kids attempted to blast automotive clerks in the ass.

When we returned home, Dad walked to the backyard and began to tape a paper target sheet onto the branch of one of the fruit trees.

"Hey, can we do this inside?" I asked nervously, wanting to keep this purchase a secret from prying eyes.

"It's a lot safer out here," Dad said. "You don't want BBs ricocheting off the walls."

"It's hot," I whined. "And I could catch Lyme disease from a mosquito, or get stung by a bee and discover that I'm allergic and swallow my tongue and choke to death!"

"Where," Dad said with a sigh as he yanked the target down, "did you learn to be so dramatic?"

We marched down to the basement, where he stuck a target onto the dartboard. Having grown up in a small Kansas town, he seemed to easily fall back into the rhythm of holding a firearm, and he taught me how to properly aim the gun.

My first several shots—not even in the vicinity of the target, but roughly on the same wall—stuck in the paneling and Dad was forced to dig them out with a penknife, whereupon he moved the dartboard to the more cramped but unpaneled laundry room, explaining that this was for my own good "so that your Mother doesn't kill you in your sleep."

As the afternoon wore on, I began to improve. I had no idea I possessed such marksman talent, landing shots within the largest target circle almost every time. By the time Mother returned from the beauty salon, Dad was no longer having to dodge BBs, although he refused to remove the towels he had placed over the washer and dryer to protect them, since any nick in the ceramic veneer would result in the summoning of the Lord Jesus to the rathskeller.

"So, what made you want to learn to shoot?" he asked.

"I want to kill one of the neighbors," I replied.

Dad chuckled. "Never can get a straight answer out of you."

OVER THE NEXT FEW WEEKS, I kept practicing, focusing the obsessive behavior I typically applied to the trumpet on hitting that target. I will, I thought, avenge that little rabbit's death. Whether there was a God or not, he obviously wasn't protecting his creations. Somebody had to.

Finally, when I was able to hit eight bull's-eyes out of ten shots, I decided it was time.

Dad had recently restrung the webbing on the aluminum patio lounge chairs, and the tight bands of scratchy plastic material served, I discovered, as a perfect support for the barrel of a gun. After carefully draping two beach towels over a chair—one of which, conveniently, had a couple of holes in it from too many washings—I aimed the chair so that its backrest—with an overhang of beach towel—perfectly hid from view a crouching marksman.

Then, I began to lie in wait.

This was, unfortunately, easier said than done. It was hot, and squatting on the redbrick patio made my thighs ache and sweat run into my eyes, blocking my vision. I was forced to take repeated breaks, missing Albert on two separate days as he trundled by, gun in one hand and red, white and blue Bomb Pop Popsicle in the other.

It was also boring. Turning a transistor radio on would only attract attention, so I had to kneel behind the chair with a paperback, alternately reading paragraphs of *Please Don't Eat the Daisies* and aiming my weapon.

By Day Five of my stakeout, things were getting seriously tedious. I hadn't seen Albert in two days, and I began to wonder if he had forsaken his homicidal ways in favor of more benign activities, like popping wheelies in the cul-de-sac or rubbing himself against his bedspread (a current favorite of mine).

My legs were sore, I'd run out of reading material and had to resort to *Popular Mechanics*, and I was missing my afternoon television reruns. But recalling the violent image of Albert and that rabbit always managed to revive my flagging contempt for this fat assassin.

Suddenly, I heard the familiar *ping*.

I quickly set down the magazine and raised my gun into position, the barrel just barely peeking through one hole of the beach towel. Albert came lumbering across the common ground, gun in hand. Where were his parents? I thought indignantly, conveniently forgetting that I was likewise unsupervised.

He stopped and glanced around, as though he heard something, giving me a perfectly stationary target. I had a fleeting moment of conscience—would shooting Albert make me no better than he? But I was immediately reminded of that biblical axiom, "An eye for an eye, a tooth for a tooth." Not that I even cared what the Bible said.

He started to move. There was no time to debate. I took aim and squeezed off a shot. *Ping!*

"Owww!!" Albert yelped, whirling around and flailing at what he obviously presumed to be a bee or a wasp.

That is for the squirrel you tried to kill, I thought as I quickly and as quietly as possible pumped the gun to reload. I took aim again. *Ping!*

"Aahhh!"

That is for the bunny you *did* kill.

Albert dropped his gun, ducking and weaving in an attempt to dodge the stinger-laden insects that he obviously thought were attacking him.

I took aim a third time. *Ping!*

That is for every other animal you've hurt or scared or just made feel unsafe.

This BB just grazed him, but it did the trick. Albert took off like a shot, back toward his house, shrieking like a big, stupid girl, leaving the gun lying conspicuously on the ground.

This was more than I could have hoped for.

I waited for thirty seconds or so to be sure that the coast was clear, then casually strode out to the edge of our backyard, glancing both ways to see if Albert was anywhere to be found. He wasn't. I grabbed his BB gun and shoved it into the waistband of my jeans, the barrel thrust down one pant leg. I pulled my shirt over the butt of the gun and slowly began to sidle nonchalantly back toward our yard.

Then I realized that if Albert came back for the gun, he might suspect I'd stolen it. His parents would confront my parents, they'd discover the evidence, and there would be a lot of screaming (Mother's) and crying (mine).

I turned and ambled as quickly as I could down the

common ground to the creek about a hundred yards away, my walk a stiff gait, what with a loaded rifle in my pants.

Some days there would be kids hanging around the creek since there was a popular rope swing suspended from one of the trees, but today, thank God, the area was empty.

I suddenly realized I hadn't really thought this through. What exactly was I gonna do with the gun?

I surveyed the area quickly. Dirt be damned, I decided. I leaped over the embankment into the stream and, in the privacy of the creek, pulled out Albert's gun and buried it as deep as possible in the mud.

I climbed back up the embankment, a filthy mess, and rushed home, quickly formulating an "I fell off the rope swing!" excuse in case Albert spotted me.

I rushed into the garage and removed all my clothing. Mud had gotten into everything, even my tighty whities. I balled the entire mess up and threw it into a Hefty bag, carrying it down to the basement. I should have enough time, I calculated, to wash and dry the clothes before Mother and Dad got home.

Unfortunately, I had no idea how to work the washer, since Mother had done every stitch of laundry in my thirteen years of life. I tossed it all into the machine and stood there naked, attempting to navigate the switches, when I heard a gasp.

"Gross!"

I froze. Val was standing behind me.

Luckily, the rope-swing excuse worked on her. She actually didn't seem to care what had happened, as long as I got some clothes on in a hurry.

And as I stood in the shower, rinsing off the mud, I felt a tremendous sense of accomplishment wash over me.

I had done this by myself.

I didn't need magic.

All I needed was me.

In the past, I might have presumed that God had somehow intervened and aided me in getting Albert's gun. But this idea now seemed wildly fanciful, a remote possibility twisted into truth only by the capricious imaginings of a boy who didn't know any better.

Yet I felt a deep and mournful longing for that magical me of the past. The teamwork that God and I had shared had been comforting. And although I was now discovering that I was strong enough to go it alone, I desperately wished that I didn't have to.

ELEVEN

The Trouble with Tids

That was private!" Val hollered, attempting to snatch my Radio Shack cassette recorder away as I played back the tape of her end of a phone conversation with her boyfriend, Tommy. "What were you doing, you little perv, holding the microphone against the *door*?"

"Of course not," I replied indignantly. "You don't get sound quality this good through a slab of wood. I hid under your bed."

I ran into my room and slammed the door, clutching the tape recorder to my chest.

"Why do you need to hear what we're talking about?!"

"Why do you need to keep it a secret?" I yelled back. "You sit in there whispering like you're plotting a murder!"

"If you play that tape for anybody," Val shrieked as she kicked the door frame, "I'll be plotting yours!"

What had happened to my relationship with my sister—the girl who once led a parade of a dozen six-year-olds down our street, naked? The girl who would unwrap and rewrap all our presents under the Christmas tree to ensure that our demands had been met? The girl who taught me how to break into the house when we came home from Vacation Bible School without our key?

We used to have such fun together, especially in the summertime. But ever since she had grown boobs (or "tids" as I now referred to them, having overheard this supercool slang term from the worldly Darren Pulaski), Val's idea of a good time seemed to revolve around making sure *I* wasn't a part of it.

She was gone all the time now. And on the rare occasion when she *was* home, she barricaded herself in her room, talking to Tommy and making collages of the name "Mrs. Tommy Kipling" from letters cut out of *Seventeen* magazine, which, even with heart-shaped *o*'s and *i*'s dotted with smiley faces, looked disturbing, and made it unclear whether her aspiration was to become a married woman or the world's youngest serial killer.

I, on the other hand, was willing to devote my time and attention to her 24/7. Truth be told, this was not so much a generosity of spirit as the fact that seventh grade had not been a good year. I hated junior high, a brick penal colony that housed all the most heinous people from elementary school plus several hundred new students vying for the title. My one class in grade school had now mutated into six classes per day, which multiplied the number of students who could despise me on a daily basis. And my only friendship—and an intermittent one at that—was with Mitch McKirby down the street, whose idea of fun was stamp collecting, a hobby so boring it almost begged to be punched.

But Val couldn't have cared less. And now, the summer days of playing Monopoly were long gone. The afternoon discussions of the pros and cons of being raised by wolves (we wouldn't have to rake the forest, but we wouldn't get paid five dollars for every A) were over. The road trips we took around the neighborhood with our pet guinea pigs in a rusted red wagon were, for Val, nothing more than a dim memory.

All because my sixteen-year-old sister had tids.

"What did you guys do today?" Dad—who was the first of our parents to arrive home each day—asked.

"I changed the guinea pigs' litter and taught Peanut

Butter how to jump up and down the stairs," I said proudly. "He's like a Slinky with fur."

"That's great," Dad said. "But make sure he doesn't do his business on the carpet. Those things are little turd machines, and if your mother finds one, she'll make you eat it."

We both laughed.

"No, I'm serious," he said. "She will." He looked around. "Where's your sister?"

"She left with Tommy and his friend Paul and I haven't seen them since. I think they mentioned something about holding up ice cream trucks. Tommy's dad has a gun."

This was, of course, patently untrue, but I'd been alone all day, Val wasn't there to hear it, and I had nothing to lose.

But no matter what kind of rumors I tried to start with Dad—"Tommy invited Val over to meet his wife"—or sympathy card I tried to play—"Not having anyone to talk to all day sure does make you wanna set fire to things"—he seemed to remain curiously blasé.

"Val's a good girl," Dad said, trying to allay my carefully rehearsed fears about her. "She's got a big, fat mouth, but she's a good girl."

In the past, I would have set to work conjuring in order to make Val realize how much she missed me. But God and I were no longer on speaking terms.

. . .

IT WAS SATURDAY NIGHT. Mother and Dad had gone out for the evening, stupidly letting slip that they wouldn't be back until eleven, an admission that, conveniently for Val, permitted the planning of carefully timed illegal activities.

"What are you doing?" I yelled, as I threw spoons at Val's bedroom door from a spot down the hallway. "Come on out. I've been working on my show. I'll give you a sneak peek!"

Over the past few weeks, I had begun creating a catalog of my own interpretations of popular songs for use in the smash hit trumpet concerts I planned to perform at stadiums all across the country. Once I was old enough to drive.

"I'd rather listen to a baby seal being clubbed to death," Val hollered from the other side of the door. "I mean, come on . . . a ballad version of 'Smokin' in the Boys' Room'?"

I heaved another utensil at the door. "It's artistic!"

"Stop bothering me, I'm getting ready!" she yelled. "Tommy's coming over."

"He can't come over without Mother and Dad here."

The door flew open.

"If you breathe a word, I'll tell Mother you were in the *living room*." She slammed the door again.

I gasped. *No one* entered the living room. No one walked on the powder blue shag carpet. No one touched the navy blue and white hand-flocked wallpaper. This room was as pristine as the day we had moved in four and a half years earlier and, like a time capsule, was destined to remain that way until the moment we would leave to live in outer space, probably in the 1980s.

"Well, that's just evil!" I heaved another utensil down the hall.

"Would you please stop throwing spoons at the door!"

"I can't do knives," I replied. "They'll leave a mark."

The doorbell rang.

With a sigh, I dropped the flatware and trudged to the front door. Tommy was standing there, looking like a teenage Jack LaLanne. He was a popular sophomore from our neighborhood who lettered in football and wrestling, and was everything I despised. His was the kind of face you wanted to smack—handsome and square-jawed, it just screamed easy confidence, and was the emblem of all that was wrong with my sister. I imagined the Rapture occurring at this moment and Jesus sucking Val and me up to Heaven, leaving Tommy standing there on the porch, looking around stupidly.

"Val here?"

It wasn't long into Val and Tommy's relationship when I determined that, of the many attributes that

Tommy supposedly possessed, conversational skill was clearly not among them. A man of three to five words, he just stood staring at me with that football hero grin. I wanted to knock him off the porch.

"Yeah, come on in," I said as I led him into the family room. Tommy flopped down on the sofa.

"You've probably figured this out," I whispered, "but it takes *hours* for her to look decent. Hope you brought a canteen and some beef jerky."

Tommy chuckled. Like most of my jokes, it was well rehearsed, since I thought of my best lines while lying around alone in my bedroom and thus had plenty of opportunity for dry runs. But Tommy didn't seem to realize it, and his amusement buoyed me a bit. It was nice having an audience.

"So," I said, "you have nine brothers and sisters?"

"Uh-huh," he grunted.

"Wow, twelve people living in one house?" I said. "What do you do, stack 'em?"

He chuckled again. "Well, there's always somebody to do stuff with."

Well, *that* was rude, I thought. I was just trying to make conversation; there was no need to be insulting. He apparently saw me as some sort of lonely, pathetic kid who didn't have any friends. I might have lost my sister, and I might not have any friends at school, but I had options. I could be looking at dusty old stamps with Mitch right now.

The door to Val's bedroom flew open again and she pranced down the hall wearing pink hot pants. I stared at her as though I were sniffing curdled milk.

"What are you looking at?" she barked at me. Then, changing gears with tire-squealing speed, she draped herself across the sofa coquettishly.

"Hi," she cooed to Tommy, as I labored to keep my potato chip and mayonnaise sandwich down. This was a side of my sister that I was unfamiliar with, this flirty, coy side, and it wasn't pretty.

"Hey," Tommy grunted, displaying his flair for conversational economy.

"So," I said brightly, clapping my hands together, "what do you guys wanna do?"

"We wanna be alone," Val replied. She pointed downstairs. "Basement or your bedroom. Your call." She plopped onto Tommy's lap and, within seconds, they were exploring each other's tonsils like Lewis and Clark.

I stood there transfixed. I had kissed a girl—Alice Larkspur—but we had not engaged in this kind of unsanitary swabbing of mouth tissues, and I found it both unsettling and kind of gross. What was the appeal of exchanging food particles and spit when I had a guinea pig downstairs who could jump entire steps in a single bound?

Val turned to me with a look that had probably killed lesser men and mouthed, "GO."

I whirled on my heel and marched to the basement steps, slamming the door behind me to make my point.

I sat in the basement fuming all the way through *All in the Family*, *Mary Tyler Moore* and *Bob Newhart*. This was unacceptable. Banishing me in my own house! Val hadn't done that since she locked me in the refrigerator when I was eight (forgetting I was there until roughly thirty seconds before—although she would argue after—brain damage set in).

Finally tiring of television, I pulled out my trumpet. *This* was a proper use of free time—developing a talent that would elevate me to the pinnacle of show business—not making out on a corduroy couch. I began to rehearse my sensitive, introspective version of "Smokin' in the Boys' Room."

As I wandered around the basement, the bell of my horn aimed at the family room where Val and Tommy sat loosening each other's fillings, I heard the stereo flip on. Val's 45 of the Brownsville Station version began blasting above my head.

"*That's* how it's supposed to sound!" she yelled.

What happened to the girl I used to spend entire afternoons baking tasty lard-laden crème puffs with?

Then it struck me, like a blinding flash of the obvious.

It wasn't the tids. It was God.

Ever since I had parted ways with the Almighty, he had been totally and deafeningly silent. I had naturally taken this as a sign of disinterest, a confirmation of his lack of caring.

But perhaps, it occurred to me now, he was stewing. And—living up to the image of the vengeful God I had been taught about in Sunday school—he was getting even with me. Since I had taken away my relationship with him, he was gonna take away mine with Val.

Well, God had done enough to me. I had suffered plenty at his hands. He was not gonna be the victor if *I* had anything to say about it.

This was war.

I BEGAN TO SEARCH for ways to get Val grounded. If I can just keep her around the house long enough, I reasoned, she'll rediscover what we once had, and we're certain to become the Two Musketeers once again.

"Does it smell like smoke in here?" I said to Dad one afternoon as I attempted to cough up a lung. "Val's switched to menthol, but it still stinks."

"Could you replace the lock on the liquor cabinet?" I asked plaintively a few days later, showing off a bruise I had gotten from running into the corner of the pool table. "Val gets mean when she drinks."

"Stop trying to get your sister in trouble," Dad said sternly, refusing to buy that his only daughter was turning into a teenage delinquent.

But I was not about to be so easily dissuaded.

"Are you guys gonna turn the den into a bedroom?" I asked a couple days later.

"Why?"

"For Val's baby. I guess she could leave it at Tommy's house. They already have ten kids, they'll never notice another one."

"Your sister is not with child," Dad said. He paused for a long moment. "Is she?"

He immediately thought better of it. Val was a good Christian girl. "Stop making up lies about your sister," he said, pointing downward. "You know what happens to liars. And we'd miss you in Heaven."

"You mean you and Mother would miss me," I corrected, although I wasn't entirely sure about Mother's status either when you got right down to it. "*Val's* gonna be too busy renting out skis at the Lake of Fire."

Dad was not turning out to be quite the patsy I had hoped, so I switched targets.

"You like my new pants?" I asked Mother as she lay sunning on the patio. I modeled the groovy new Wranglers I had secretly asked Val to purchase with her employee discount at Kmart. "Val shoplifted 'em. If you need anything, I'm sure she could help you out."

Mother slowly lifted her goggles to take a look.

"Your sister gave me the receipt," she said matter-of-factly.

"She must have forged it," I replied nervously.

"I wouldn't put anything past her. She'll probably be counterfeiting twenties by senior year."

"Let me know if she graduates to fifties," Mother said as she replaced the goggles. "I could use a few of those."

MY FRUSTRATION WAS GROWING. How could no one see that grounding this girl would be the best thing for everyone involved?

Val was staying away from home even more now, and the summer days dragged on like a prison sentence. I had perfected my concert, but had no one to perform it for. I had afternoon reruns of *Gilligan's Island* and *The Munsters*, but no one to watch them with. I had blank cassette tapes to record on, but no one to blackmail.

Then, one afternoon, as I stood in the basement rehearsing the curtain calls for my concert (using the roar of applause from Judy Garland's Carnegie Hall album as my cue to return to the stage), an opportunity presented itself on a silver platter.

I heard voices overhead.

I slipped upstairs to find that Val, Tommy and Tommy's best friend Paul had shown up. Paul was a similarly slack-jawed jock who was so muscular he appeared to have been blown up with a tire pump. With only one operating ear, I had always been bad at placing sounds, but as I eavesdropped, it seemed as though their voices were coming from the living room.

Of course, that was impossible. I crept into the foyer. But the closer I got, the more obvious it became that, indeed, they were in the living room.

I peered around the corner. Paul was sprawled across the white crushed velvet love seat, his leg hanging over one arm. Val was curled up against Tommy on the matching white crushed velvet sofa, her bare feet touching the cushion.

My head began to spin. What was Val thinking? Was she becoming the delinquent I had attempted to paint her as? Had the tids turned her into a felon?

It was a boiling hot day outside. I stifled a gasp as I watched Tommy and Paul's sweat stain the virgin fabrics, their dirty tennis shoes resting on the expensive wood and marble coffee table as if this were somebody's cheesy rec room and not the Poole altar of high style.

I was almost giddy with anticipation.

I hightailed it to my bedroom. I could hear them talking and laughing as I grabbed my new 110 Instamatic and tiptoed to the foyer once again, edging up to the corner of the wall.

My hands were shaking, my heart beating wildly. This was, I reasoned, a necessary evil, a take-no-prisoners step that would force my sister back into the sibling fold, where she belonged.

I took a deep breath and, as fast as I could, swiveled around the corner.

"Smile!" I yelled, centering Val and Tommy in the viewfinder and clicking the shutter. The flash cube *poofe*d as a wild-eyed Val jumped up.

"Oh, no you don't!" she yelled. I scampered into my bedroom, slamming the door behind me. "Gimme that camera, you little weasel!"

I dropped onto the floor, using the bed as leverage to keep my full weight holding the door shut.

"Mother's gonna kill you!" I sang in a singsong voice.

Val turned the knob, throwing her weight against the door, screaming like a banshee.

"If you develop that picture, you won't live to see fourteen!"

"Oh, I'm gonna develop it, all right," I said, "and you're gonna be grounded until the Second Coming!"

"Oh yeah?!" She banged on the door.

"Yeah!"

I paused for effect. "But maybe," I said slyly, "I could be convinced to make a deal."

"Like what?"

"I won't show Mother the picture," I said, panting as I continued to hold the door shut, "if you let me perform my whole trumpet concert for you."

"Oh God, why don't you just kill me?"

"What?" I said defensively. "I'm not so bad!"

She had now forced the door far enough open to get

233

one leg into the bedroom, and as she pressed against the door, she softened. "I never said you were. Actually, I guess I've never told you this, but . . . I think you're pretty talented."

I smiled—and momentarily let my guard down. With her foot, Val kicked me in the shin and I tumbled over, the door falling open. She tried to grab the camera. I shoved it down my pants.

"You're dead meat!" she shrieked.

I smiled triumphantly, daring her to go for the camera, knowing that she wouldn't. We were not the type of people who touched each other *there*.

"GOD IN HEAVEN!!"

I smiled. Dad must have just showed Mother the picture. Suddenly, I thought, all those accusations I had made about Val were doubtless being seen in a new light. They'd probably start ransacking her room for empty gin bottles, checking her teeth for nicotine stains and waiting for her water to break. She would be home with me for the rest of the summer and possibly the entire school year to come.

From my bedroom, I heard footsteps stomping down the hall. Mother burst into Val's room.

"That room is for company!" she shrieked at a decibel level that thoughtfully allowed the participation of the entire neighborhood.

"Tommy *is* company!" Val yelled back, albeit with far less conviction.

"Company," Mother bellowed, "is people we want to impress. Company is people we probably don't even like. Company is not any *teenager* in the known universe!"

"We were just relaxing!"

I had a momentary flash of regret. Val was basically a law-abiding citizen. Should she really be punished for this one felonious act?

Fortunately, my sister—who had never quite gotten the hang of rolling over and playing dead—resolved my dilemma.

"You relax on a lawn chair, not on crushed velvet!" Mother snapped.

"Well, it's already crushed, what's the big friggin' deal?"

Within another thirty seconds, Val was grounded for a week.

And I was elated. I not only didn't need God, I was beating him at his own game.

IT WAS DAY THREE of Val's Incarceration.

Although she had spent the past year refining her skills as a recluse whenever at home (a sort of Howard Hughes with tids), this was different. Her obsession with Tommy could not be indulged this week, since part of her grounding was a ban on telephone use, and I was charged with policing this activity.

This necessitated a lot of intensive surveillance, watching TV with the sound off in order to detect the rotary dialing of the phone, and quietly lifting the receiver every few minutes to ensure that there was nothing more than a dial tone. But it was worth it, since she had little else to occupy herself in there, and was, I was certain, getting stir-crazy.

The bedroom door flew open. Val marched down the hall.

"Hey," I said from the family room, "I need your advice."

"Leave me alone." The bathroom door slammed shut.

"Peanut Butter's getting fat!" I hollered, referring to my athletic little stair-jumper.

Val had lost interest in our longtime pets some time ago, and she visited them in their basement box infrequently now, so she was unaware that Peanut Butter was turning into a rodent Dom DeLuise.

"So what?" she yelled from the bathroom.

"It's not healthy! What do I do?"

"Make him do laps around the pool table," she snapped. "What do I care?"

I crept up to the bathroom door. "I'm sorry," I said hesitantly, "for getting you in trouble."

"You should be. Nobody likes a snitch. And you wonder why you don't have any friends."

"I have friends," I said defensively. "Mitch down the street."

The door flew open. "Yeah, that's something to be proud of. He's a bigger freak than you are." She pushed past me and walked into the kitchen.

"I could have other friends," I retorted. "There just aren't very many people on my level."

"Well, maybe," she replied as she grabbed a glass bottle of Coke from the refrigerator, "you should consider lowering your standards. You wanna be stuck in the house for the rest of your life?"

"It's not so bad. I mean, you and I could do something."

"Like what?"

"We could play Monopoly."

She snorted. "Oh, please."

"I'll let you steal money from the bank."

"Eric," she said patiently as she poured a glass of soda, "I'm going on seventeen. You're thirteen. We don't like to do the same things."

"Well then, what do *you* want to do?" I said, anxiety coloring my voice. I could feel my control of the situation slipping away.

"I wanna go see Tommy."

"Well, I could go, too. We could hang out together."

"Tommy likes you," she said, chuckling, "but not *that* much."

I felt my face grow red. I turned away.

Val replaced the bottle in the refrigerator. "I'm sorry," she said. "It's not you. I'm just older now. I like different things."

She turned to walk back to her bedroom.

"I could let you go see him," I blurted out.

She stopped. "You'd do that for me?"

"Sure," I said hesitantly, feeling alternately grown-up and deceitful. "What's the big deal?"

VAL MADE ME promise that I wouldn't rat her out. In exchange, she brought me back a 45 I'd been wanting, Paul Anka's "You're Havin' My Baby."

I had won some measure of respect and gratitude from my sister. But it was a hollow victory. There seemed to be no going back to the way we once were.

"Okay," I said to God as I set Peanut Butter down next to the pool table and nudged him forward to begin his laps. "You win."

THE NEXT DAY, as I was practicing my trumpet, Val clomped downstairs.

"Would you turn that thing down a little?!" she said. "I can't even hear myself think."

"I can hear you thinking from all the way over here," I replied. "Those gears need some oil."

Val started to reply. Fighting wasn't much, but at least it was engagement.

Suddenly, I held my finger to my lips to shush her.

For all the years we had had our guinea pigs, the mere opening of the door to the basement triggered a chorus of squeals. It had suddenly hit me that Val had just thrown open the door and pounded down the stairs with nary a sound from them.

I ran across the basement to the laundry room.

Oh God, oh God, I thought, terror filling my body, you already won. Please let that be enough.

I dashed into the corner and looked into the guinea pigs' box. Peanut Butter was writhing, obviously in pain. Mickey, his companion, was sitting there watching quietly.

It was the laps, I thought. The torture I had inflicted on him. The strain on his portly little body did him in. Tears filled my eyes.

Val walked in.

"What's the problem?"

I pointed. She leaned over and gasped.

"Gross!"

Her insensitivity to the suffering of my beloved pet infuriated me.

"*Shut up!* He can't help it!"

"Well, of course he can't," Val said. "Look!"

She pointed and I hesitantly glanced into the box again.

Peanut Butter was having a baby.

"Ewww!" I yelled, both repulsed and overjoyed. Peanut Butter shuddered in pain and whimpered.

"Oh my God," Val said, a look of disgust on her face, "I am *never* doing that!"

We gazed quietly at the scene playing out before us. We had never had baby *anythings*.

"Well," Val said softly, "I guess those aerobics did the trick."

"Well," I said softly, "I guess he's a she."

Slowly, one, then two new guinea pigs took their places in the box. They looked like tiny, hairless lumps.

"Where's their fur?" I asked.

"It grows in later, I guess."

"Look at their feet," I said. "They're so little."

"And their eyes," Val whispered. "They're closed. I wonder when they open?"

A third baby made its way onto the scene.

"How many has she got in there?" I asked. "It's like a pastry tube."

"I don't know." She pointed to Mickey, who I now realized was the father. "Look how quiet he is."

"Guess he's just glad it's not him, huh?"

"Either that, or he's goin', 'How am I gonna pay for all these kids?'"

We both laughed. I reached down. "Can we pick 'em up?"

Val stopped my hand. "We probably shouldn't. We don't wanna get human stink on 'em so that she rejects them or eats them or something."

"Would she do that?" I asked, horrified.

Val nodded knowingly. "We should probably go upstairs and let them sleep."

"Will she be okay by herself?" I asked. I had to get used to this new pronoun thing.

"She got this far without our help," Val replied. "I think she'll be just fine."

We tiptoed upstairs, the thrill of new life filling us with a civility we hadn't shown each other in a very long time.

And I silently—albeit hesitantly—thanked God. I certainly wasn't convinced that he was in my corner, but for at least this one moment, he had given me my sister back.

"Hey," I said to Val, before she could head down the hall to her room, "you wanna watch *Bewitched*?"

There was a long pause. Too long. I steeled myself for the answer.

"Oh, jeez," she said, rolling her eyes, her hands on her hips. She gazed at me for a moment, as if taking in my pained expression but more likely calculating the cost/benefit ratio. "Well . . ." she replied, "I guess."

I beamed.

"But don't be waving your arms around when Endora comes on," she said as she plopped down on the family room shag and flipped on the Zenith. "That's weird."

TWELVE

Frogface

Fifth-period Social Studies was no place for mortals.

This class, held in one of the double-wide trailers situated behind Hazelwood Junior High, was a uniquely designed torture chamber where no one could hear you scream.

The trailers were intended to ease overcrowding, the result of a large Catholic population that seemed to believe that a family wasn't really a family if it couldn't staff an entire Sambo's restaurant or a community theater production of *Hello, Dolly!* What these trailers bred instead was an enthusiastic strain of sadism. Separated from the main building, where the potential for the discovery of misconduct was much higher, the trailers were a spring training camp for budding Marquises de Sade. A place where only the magically inclined could survive.

Unfortunately, I was still not at all certain that God was in my corner. Any link between me and the powerful Endora of my magical past was tenuous at best. And my eighth-grade classmates, many of whom were undergoing rigorous instruction in ruthlessness, had apparently been notified. Wholly aware of my inability to counteract their cruelty, they launched attacks that were impressive in both scope and nuance.

Black Kenny, for example—one of the school's few kids of (any) color—felt that book removal should be scored on a point system: one point for knocking them out of my hands; two points for broadcasting the breaking news that I carried them like a girl; three points if he was subsequently able to heave them out the window into the mud. Six points was a slow week; eight points a respectable one; ten, worthy of commendation and a plaque.

In a rare show of unity, members of the school's burnout contingent shared in the persecution duties. Willy Fleming, whose sex appeal was somewhat incongruous to his status as a burnout, favored a form of physical intimidation that violated all rules of personal space. Standing mere inches from my face, Willy would flip the ends of my hair, which, in the aquatic Missouri humidity, tended to curl up, thus giving me an uncanny resemblance to Marlo Thomas in *That Girl*.

"Hey, CessPoole," he would whisper menacingly, reprising a nickname I had striven for years to lose, "where's your boyfriend *Donald*?" He was alluding, of course, to Marlo's on-screen beau from the 1960s TV series. I considered advising him that the show had gone off the air several years earlier, and if he wanted to be a successful comic, he might consider topicality, but thought better of it.

His fingers flicked my hair again, as a cadre of swooning girls began to play with their split ends.

"I know," I would reply lamely. "My stupid hair. What're ya gonna do?"

It was this sort of snappy comeback that ensured repeat performances, so each day I counted down the moments until the arrival of our teacher, Miss Plotnick, whose whereabouts prior to the beginning of class were a mystery, although she was apparently not in the bathroom dolling up.

Miss Plotnick was a short, slightly dumpy woman of perhaps thirty, whose wide, squat moonface made it appear as though her head had been smashed like Wile E. Coyote's in a Roadrunner cartoon. This, at least, seemed to be the widely held belief of Willy and Black Kenny, who announced that no amount of makeup or JCPenney pantsuits could assuage the fact that she had been beaten senseless with an ugly stick.

I, on the other hand, thought she was beautiful— inside, where it counted. Because contrary to her students, Miss Plotnick liked me.

"Quiet, everyone," she would announce, clapping her hands, her mousy brown hair flapping like a dead squirrel. "Today we're going to role-play the branches of government!"

Everyone moaned. Miss Plotnick was a fan of lessons that encouraged some form of interactivity. Her valiant efforts to teach us stuff using games like Current Events Jeopardy usually failed miserably; but like Sisyphus, she continued to push that educational boulder up the trailer.

"Let's see . . ." She glanced around the room with the breathless anticipation of Bob Barker announcing the Showcase Showdown winner. "I'd like *Eric* to play the Executive Branch."

Black Kenny (who, oddly, seemed to have a chip on his shoulder about being called Black Kenny, although it was really just a means of differentiating him from the regular Kenny) immediately piped up. "What do you want *that* fairy for?"

Several kids tittered as Miss Plotnick whirled around to him.

"One more comment like that, Kenny, and you're gonna be in detention until you're forty." She turned back to me. "I'm choosing Eric because he seems so presidential," she announced with a conviction borne of no evidence.

Although pleased to be singled out for her affection, attention was really the last thing I wanted. As someone who was already a target, keeping my head down was a priority, since being teacher's pet would bring me nothing so much as a season pass to an ass kicking.

Nonetheless, I quietly took a seat behind her desk, which served as the Oval Office, and, at her urging, began issuing executive orders, as the students performing the roles of the Judicial and Legislative branches argued that "Bring me my enemies list!" was not in their job description.

"Perhaps Richard Nixon isn't the president you would most want to emulate," Miss Plotnick said kindly, noting that impeachment wouldn't be the sort of thing you highlight on a job résumé. "But," she added as I dashed back to my desk, "you definitely have the potential to be a leader!"

Black Kenny made a face. Willy threw a spitball at me. Several girls fluffed their hair and crumpled up bits of paper—on which they'd been practicing writing "Mrs. Willy Fleming"—and offered them to him as subsequent missiles.

"The toad and the CessPoole," Black Kenny whispered, nodding at Miss Plotnick and me. "Figures they'd like each other."

At this point in my junior high career, popularity seemed out of the question, a goal as unattainable as understanding football. I longed simply to be accepted by my peers, to be afforded the same general disregard by the bullies as ninety-five percent of the student body.

There was, unfortunately, no way I could see to make that happen. Much as I longed to believe that magic was still possible, I had little evidence of it. Endora's powers seemed to exist only in a make-believe world. And this world was all too real.

"For Friday," Miss Plotnick said, pausing by my desk, "I'd like each of you to create a family 'archaeology.'"

Doreen Hooper, who sat in front of me, raised her hand.

"You want us to dig up somebody who's dead?"

Miss Plotnick sighed. "No, dear. I want you each to bring in some small artifacts from home that represent the members of your family. You know, pictures, little trinkets, that kind of thing. I'm going to bring in soil, and we'll 'bury' them in the dirt for your classmates to uncover and decipher. This will help us create a microcosm of American society."

Everyone moaned.

"Eric, your father works for McDonnell-Douglas, doesn't he? Maybe you could bring in a picture of an airliner. That sort of thing."

Doreen raised her hand again.

"My father owns a car dealership," she announced as though this were news to anyone there. "Should I bring in the keys for a new Chevrolet?"

Doreen was a founding member of the "Elites"—those popular students who were destined to go on to be cheerleaders and quarterbacks in high school (thus, I imagined, assuring them a lifetime of acclaim). She was beautiful, dumb as a stump, and so popular she probably could have bombed the school and gotten off with detention. She wore so much Charlie perfume that my stomach was on evacuation alert on a daily basis; but since she had never participated in the Daily Degradathon, I kept a small bottle of Pepto-Bismol handy in a courageous show of team spirit.

"Only things you can spare, dear," Miss Plotnick replied, "since they'll be covered with dirt for a while."

"Wonder if we could cover *her* with dirt," Black Kenny whispered, referring to Miss Plotnick. "It'd make it a whole lot easier on our eyes."

Several kids nervously laughed, afraid not to, but worried, since Black Kenny's volume control was routinely set on 8. Miss Plotnick glanced up, yet didn't appear to hear him, and he sat back with a satisfied smile.

You're not ugly, I thought, gazing at Miss P. You're just like Barbra Streisand—you have a special beauty that stupid bullies aren't equipped to appreciate.

Doreen turned around to me. "Hey, Eric."

I was stunned. We had sat six inches apart for months, yet I was certain that Doreen was unaware of my existence, since she had never, until now, acknowledged it.

"Would you help me think of some things I could use for my brother? He's like you."

Doreen Hooper was talking to me. Doreen Hooper wanted my help!

Enthralled by this sudden and unwarranted personal attention, I spent several glorious minutes after the bell conferring with her about her brother, who drew sketches of women in evening gowns and whom she had repeatedly caught performing numbers from the musical *Cabaret*. What this had to do with me was a mystery, but no matter. I was talking to an Elite—and people saw me.

I sagely suggested a fabric swatch (for the sketches) or a hairbrush (for the microphone). Doreen thanked me and smiled. I could not believe my good fortune.

I fairly floated out of the classroom, and spent the next several afternoons carefully assembling my archaeology with the kind of items that might impress both a teacher and a certain Elite—while avoiding the ridicule of everyone else. For Dad, I had a photo of an F-15 jet fighter and a bottle of Old Spice cologne. For Val, a Grand Funk Railroad 45 and a mood ring. For Mother, a brand-new can of Comet and a wine list.

I approached Archaeology Day with a combination

of anticipation and trepidation, since this class could, given my luck, go either way. I held my bag tightly as I marched into the trailer, quickly scanning the room for Willy and Black Kenny, both of whom were fortunately busy with their own accoutrements and could not be bothered, today, with destroying mine.

I took a deep breath and feigned an air of casual confidence. "Hey, Dor," I said loudly to Doreen as I sat down, using the nickname I had heard her fellow Elites use, "did you find the stuff for your brother?"

"What?" she said without turning around, busy evaluating her lip gloss with a compact mirror. "Oh. No," she said, snapping the compact shut. "I just did my parents."

Perhaps the fabric swatch was too complicated, I thought. I should have given her something easier, like a top hat or the *Cabaret* soundtrack—things everyone has.

Miss Plotnick, who was smoothing out the dirt in a large metal tub on her desk, removed her gardening gloves and clapped her hands.

"Okay, class, let's get started. As you bring your items up, I'll select one to put in the tub for this first round. Then I'll mix them up so that they'll be chosen randomly, and we'll discuss what that item signifies."

Row by row, we deposited trinkets in the tub. Miss Plotnick selected the small bottle of Old Spice cologne as my first item (to my dismay, since I had mentally rehearsed an elaborate explanation for the F-15 photo), carefully sifting it in with the other items in the tub. She then began to choose students one by one to pull an article from the tub, as we discussed whose parent or grandparent or newly discovered bastard sibling the item belonged to and what it meant for society as a whole.

Doreen pulled out a photo of a small black child.

"I'm gonna say"—she surveyed the room exhaustively, although we only had one black kid in the class—"that this is . . . Black Kenny's brother." She exhibited a dazzling smile of accomplishment.

"We don't refer to people by their color, Doreen," Miss Plotnick said sternly. "That's what I want us to discuss. Labels marginalize us. How would you like it if we called you 'White Doreen'?"

"Go for it," Doreen said. "I'm not ashamed."

"Great job, Dor," I whispered collegially. Doreen smiled.

As Miss Plotnick labored to explain the concept of racial inequality, she began to frown and wrinkle her nose. Doreen and I were, of course, clueless to what she was smelling, since Doreen's Charlie precluded the detection of any other scent within a five-mile radius.

"What *is* that?" Miss Plotnick finally muttered aloud, moving the items around.

Suddenly she gasped. "Oh, good heavens!"

Apparently, I had failed to realize that the stopper

in the bottle of Dad's Old Spice cologne was loose; and as she had sifted through the items, the cologne had tipped over, slowly turning the tub of photos and other paraphernalia into a fragrantly spicy stew.

"Someone run to the bathrooms and grab some paper towels!"

Four or five kids, seizing on this opportunity to be sprung from class, dashed out the door as she dug through the pile.

"Whose was this?" Miss Plotnick demanded, holding up the bottle. "It leaked all over everything!"

Everyone gasped. Various kids dashed up to the front to pull their items out of the muddy mess as Miss Plotnick grabbed a handkerchief from her purse and attempted to clean them.

"Well?!"

Slowly, I raised my hand.

Willy snorted. "Retard!" he hollered as the girls around him laughed (as attractively as possible).

Doreen turned around to me. "If you messed up those car keys," she shouted, "you just bought yourself a Monte Carlo!"

Miss Plotnick sighed as she attempted to salvage various items. "It's not your fault, Eric. I put the bottle in there. I guess I should have checked it more closely."

"Yeah, he was just trying to make Plotnick feel at home," Black Kenny stage-whispered from the back row as two of the missing kids came running back in with paper towels. "Don't all toads like swamps?"

Even with one operable ear, I found this hard to miss. Fortunately, Miss Plotnick seemed to be so consumed with the circle of kids snatching muddy objects and shrieking that their mothers were going to kill them that she was oblivious to what came next.

"So," Black Kenny announced with fanfare, as though an actual 100-watt bulb had lit up over his head at his latest thought, "I wonder how *Frogface* likes her swamp?"

The creation of nicknames for teachers was, of course, a popular and beloved pastime, and many others had names almost as insulting—"Hitler," "Caveman," "Whiskey Pete"—but they were mean teachers who deserved their labels. Miss Plotnick was nice. And she couldn't help her looks.

Miss Plotnick seemed pained. Obviously, I had ruined Archaeology Day.

It was no longer a question as to which way fifth period would go. My classmates were pissed at me. Doreen thought I was an idiot. And my folly had given rise to a nickname for which I felt at least partially responsible.

As I rode the bus home to a derisive refrain of "Way to go, CessPoole," from several female members of Willy's Greek chorus, I wished I were eight again. Young enough to believe in magic. Young enough to think I could change my world. But I was a teenager now, older and wiser about the bleak realities of life.

I was a bigger pariah than ever. And Miss Plotnick was now, simply, Frogface.

"DID YOU HEAR?" Black Kenny whispered a couple of weeks later. "Frogface is getting a new lily pad!" The nickname had swept the class like wildfire, and nearly every day since its inception, someone had come in with a new bon mot that they had slaved over the night before in lieu of actual homework.

Fortunately, Miss Plotnick seemed to have been none the wiser.

At least, until now.

Doreen had not spoken to me since the archaeology incident. Nor had anyone else, of course, with the exception of Willy, who had stopped calling me "CessPoole" and shifted to the simpler and more conversationally economical "'Tard"; and Black Kenny, who thoughtfully took the time to inform me that by getting Old Spice on the picture of his baby brother, I was living on borrowed time.

"This week, class," Miss Plotnick began, "we're going to pretend that there's been a nuclear war. Won't that be fun?"

"Can we pick who gets to die?" Black Kenny shouted. "I nominate CessPoole."

The class erupted in laughs—led, to my horror, by Doreen—as Miss Plotnick grabbed Kenny by the collar to haul him to the principal's office.

Yet more painful than the certain death that awaited me at Black Kenny's hands was my swift and blood-curdling fall from Elite grace. For one brief, shining moment, I had been a friend of Doreen Hooper's. I had been Almost Popular.

"God," Doreen said to Linda, an Elite who sat next to her, as we awaited Miss P's return, "she has *no* sense of humor."

"*Zero,*" I said, craning my neck toward them, desperate to regain my Slightly Elite status, forgetting that Kenny's joke involved my untimely demise. "She just doesn't get it." I laughed conspiratorially, unaware that the trailer door had opened. "But then," I added, "what would you expect from a Frogface? Ribbit!"

I suddenly realized that the room was quiet. And that Miss Plotnick was standing next to me.

"What did you call me?"

I shrunk back, horrified. "Oh, uh, n-n-nothing. I was just joking around."

"What. Did. You. Call me."

I looked down. "Frogface."

Miss Plotnick stood over me for a moment. The room was crackling with anticipation, both of Miss P's reaction and the terms of what would doubtless be a singularly devastating punishment.

The only time I had been sent to the principal's office was the previous year, for chewing gum in class, and it had resulted in three days of after-school imprisonment with a group of kids who were destined to consider Leavenworth just a rest stop on the freeway to Folsom. I had learned from that experience why criminals—surrounded by bad influences while incarcerated—often remained criminals, and wondered if, this time, I would be unable to resist the forces of evil, and would be knocking over dry cleaners by the time I got out.

But even greater than my concern for the punishment that awaited me was my mortification that I had hurt someone so deeply. Particularly someone who had been so kind to me.

I was afraid to look up at Miss Plotnick, so I simply stared down at the cheap blond wood grain of the desktop and awaited her cold, harsh words.

But there were none. She was obviously angry, but she returned to her desk and ordered us to read aloud, one at a time, from our textbook, while she sat gazing down at her teacher's manual with a blank, faraway expression.

MISS PLOTNICK NEVER disciplined me, and in the weeks following my Frogface faux pas, my popularity began to grow. My classmates saw me as a renegade, a loose cannon, someone to be respected and feared. I had insulted a teacher to her face and gotten away with it. I was Hazelwood's own Dirty Harry. Okay, perhaps not Dirty Harry, but a détente had definitely set in. Willy and his admirers ignored me. Black Kenny, having gotten wind of my bravado while in detention, had magnanimously called off the hit. Even Doreen began acknowledging my existence again.

Of course, the pressure was on to repeat my behavior, to prove that I was a bona fide rebel. But hadn't I done enough damage? Although Miss Plotnick had not sent me to the principal's office, she wasn't speaking to me, either, and I felt her pain grow a bit each day. The "Frogface" nickname had taken on a life of its own, in passed notes and quiet whispers and jokes told outside the trailer. She seemed to be aware of the growing buzz and, slowly but surely, was withdrawing into herself. Her lessons had mutated into more book readings and pop quizzes, the standard stuff teachers seemed to favor to keep us busy while they read Harlequin romance novels. She rarely smiled. She never called on me.

I desperately wished that I could magically make it all better. But I couldn't. God might have given me a momentary reprieve with my sister, but the days of waving my arms and completely changing my destiny were gone.

. . .

As my popularity continued to swell, the con-
flict inside me grew worse.

I attempted to maintain my anarchist image by
nicknaming my geometry teacher "Bonehead Brown."
A heavyset, middle-aged man with a blond crew cut
and a distinct distaste for kids, Mr. Brown spent most
of his time giving us tests, the answers for which we
were allowed to check—on the honor system—against
his teacher's manual, which he left open on his desk.
There was, naturally, no such thing as an honor system
among eighth-graders, and the class spawned an aston-
ishing number of A students, which was fine by Bonehead, since he never wanted to see us again, anyway.

Bonehead had it coming, I rationalized. But a
thought continued to nag at the back of my mind:
Miss Plotnick didn't.

It was the afternoon of our last day before Eas-
ter break. After the bell rang and my classmates performed their ritualistic dash for the door as though
the trailer was a grenade whose pin had just been
pulled, I lingered at my desk, ostensibly finishing up
some notes in my blue spiral notebook. When everyone had gone, and before any sixth-period students
could wander in, I slipped up to Miss Plotnick's desk.

"Miss Plotnick?" My voice came out as a hoarse
whisper. I cleared my throat nervously. "Miss Plotnick?"

She was grading a paper and didn't look up. "What, Eric?" she said flatly.

"If you're too busy, I can—"

She set her pen down with a sigh, but still didn't look up at me. "What is it?"

"Ummm," I began, "you probably don't even remember this, but a few weeks back I said this stupid thing about you, and—"

"I remember." She looked up at me with an expression I couldn't quite read. Was she angry? Disappointed? Annoyed? "You know, Eric . . . I've come to expect mean words from the other kids. But you—you're better than that."

I looked down. "I'm sorry."

"Why would you do that to me?"

I stared at my feet. "I don't know."

"Oh, I suspect you do," she said. "And it would behoove you to think about whether what you've gained is real or illusory."

"What's 'illusory'?"

"Look it up."

As I paced around the basement, I opened my dictionary.

"Illusory . . ." I read to myself. "Deceptive. False. Not real."

Did she mean that what I got by hurting her was fake? That was, quite simply, absurd. I was now somewhat popular, almost looked up to. I had *never* meant to hurt her, but the results of that mistake were nothing short of a miracle. I had gotten a taste of the good life.

How can I make Miss Plotnick feel better, I wondered, but still maintain my Bad Boy image?

Magic didn't seem like a really viable option. I no longer had my bedspread, and God and I were barely on speaking terms.

But I had nowhere else to turn. And nothing to lose.

I sat down in the elderly rocking chair in which I had spent most of my basement-bound life, and closed my eyes. I began to envision the teacher that I used to know—the smiling, animated Miss Plotnick, the teacher who tried to engage us, who tried to make learning fun.

"Umm, God . . ." I said silently. "After everything that's happened, I don't really expect anything magical from you. But maybe if you could just listen."

AN IDEA WASN'T long in coming.

That night, I knelt over my bed and took out a piece of the engraved stationery that Mother and Dad had given to me as a birthday present. Laying it across a Carpenters album as my writing tablet, I began to compose.

"Dear Miss Plotnick," I wrote in my best cursive, "I am so sorry. I didn't mean to make fun of you. I just wanted to be liked. I'm sure you can understand this, being somebody who probably wasn't liked, either. But I know how it feels to have your feelings hurt, and it sure isn't fun. I hope you will forgive me. Your admirer, Eric Poole."

MISS PLOTNICK NEVER acknowledged the note, which I slipped into her desk drawer the next afternoon when no one was looking. But it didn't matter. It worked. Slowly but surely, she began to smile at me again in class.

My heart filled with hope. Had God actually answered my plea?

Then, Miss Plotnick began to call on me. There seemed to be *something* otherworldly at work, here.

Then, somewhat disturbingly, she began to treat me as though I were her most beloved, star pupil, taking pains to single me out in almost every situation.

If this was God's handiwork, it wasn't funny.

Kenny was the first to notice. (I had dropped the "Black" as part of my rebel campaign, calling him simply "Kenny" to indicate our brotherhood, which, for reasons that eluded me, he had actually seemed to like.) He immediately reinstated his book-removal activities, knocking my textbooks out of my hands with set-your-watch regularity.

Doreen once again began to forget that anyone sat behind her, rediscovering my existence only when she had a question about why her brother wanted ballet slippers for his birthday.

Then Willy returned to his name-calling—but rather than "CessPoole" or " 'Tard," he developed a new name, one that spoke to my new role as Miss Plotnick's lapdog.

"Hey, *Pet*," he sneered, exhibiting his astonishingly marginal creativity, "meet me behind the school at three. I'm gonna beat the living crap out of you."

When the bell rang that afternoon, I hung back, waiting for the last of my classmates to clear out. Miss Plotnick noticed my reluctance to leave.

"Is something wrong, Eric?"

"Sort of," I said hesitantly, unsure how to broach the subject. She walked down the row and sat down at Doreen's desk.

"What's up?"

"Well," I began, "I'll probably be dead by nightfall, so this might not matter . . ."

"But you want me to stop calling on you so much."

I looked up at her, startled.

"You don't want the kids thinking you're teacher's pet. Am I right?"

I nodded. How on earth had she figured this out?

Since she wasn't beautiful, were her other senses heightened?

"Eric," she said quietly, "do you see what I meant now? You were only popular because you were pretending to be someone you're not. The minute you became who you really are once again, the popularity you thought you had disappeared."

She looked me in the eye.

"That doesn't mean you don't deserve to be popular, because you do. Just don't bother trying to earn it with these idiots. Be yourself. Let the people who appreciate that find *you*. And they will."

She squeezed my hand and got up and returned to her desk.

IF GOD WAS INVOLVED in this, he had decided to teach me a lesson. Perfect. Because I hadn't had enough of those. I was grateful that Miss Plotnick was no longer hurt, but what was the point of forgiveness if I was dead?

Sure, I could sneak off campus and evade Willy today, but it was pointless to try—sooner or later, I'd have to pay the piper.

"Dear God," I whispered as I walked the last mile to our three-o'clock showdown. "I sure don't understand why you grant some magical requests and not others . . . but if you were in the mood to save a life right now, I wouldn't mind if it were mine."

As I turned the corner of the building, I stopped short. A fist was aimed directly at my face. I gasped.

"*Gotcha*, Pet." Willy laughed.

I chuckled weakly. Was this how death would come? A single blow to the brain? I really should have written down some songs for my funeral service, I thought, like "You Are the Sunshine of My Life" and "Alone Again, Naturally," so Mother and Dad would know what songs to play to make people cry.

"You're probably wondering why I called this meeting," he said casually, chewing a big wad of Dubble Bubble.

"Not really," I replied. "It was pretty clear."

"I'm a busy guy," he said, obviously referring to his full schedule of intimidation and shakedowns. "And I'm offering you the chance to do all my Social Studies homework. Isn't that great?"

Pinch me, I thought.

He stared at me, smiling. What was he waiting for? I closed my eyes and thought back to Tim, my grade-school bully, and how I had overcome him. Why didn't I have the courage to overcome Willy? Please, God, I begged silently, let death come swiftly.

"Don't you get it?"

I opened my eyes. Willy was still smiling, his fist by his side.

"If you're doing my homework," Willy said, "you're still alive."

. . .

THAT AFTERNOON, a deal was struck. And Willy began to protect me. In exchange for doing his homework, he was willing to be seen with me, at least occasionally. And he kept Kenny off my back.

The combination of Miss Plotnick's heralding of my intellectual abilities and my no longer being the bull's-eye in the bullies' target began to draw a few other kids to me. And very slowly, I started to make a friend or two. It was no sea change in my status like I had experienced before, but it was something. And this time, it was honestly earned. Other than the passing-my-work-off-as-Willy's part.

And I began to think that there might just be a method to God's magic. Maybe he was still with me. Maybe he did grant requests. And maybe I should accept the magic he did grant with the knowledge that something larger was at work.

But it sure would be easier if I'd just been born an Elite.

THIRTEEN

Blow, Gabriel, Blow

H ey, Cafeteria Queer."

I don't know what I'd been thinking. Throughout much of my freshman year at Hazelwood Central Senior High, I had eaten my noontime meal in the band room or at home—safe havens where I could avoid giving the bully brigade the opportunity to exercise a level of creativity that they justifiably considered far too precious and fleeting to waste on homework assignments.

On this day, however, I had decided to test the theory that, as a sophomore who'd proven myself as a committed member of several of the school's bands— bands that supported the football team and backed the performers of the spring musical, for God's sake—surely I was now viewed as integral to the fabric of the school. Perhaps even a sparkling rhinestone in that fabric.

"We don't allow queers in the cafeteria."

Tony Tropler and his gang of made men stood next to the table at which I sat with my friend Mitch McKirby, a bandmate whose hobbies of playing the clarinet and stamp collecting should, by all rights, have had Tony virtually calling dibs on him.

Without missing a beat, Mitch waved at someone in the distance who wasn't there, picked up his tray and scurried off. I couldn't blame him.

"I'm no queer," I said, laughing with him at this ridiculous label.

"Wait, I got another one," Tony said to his friends, obviously auditioning material for a new stand-up routine. "Hey, Lunch Lady. Where's your hairnet?"

The friends snickered and elbowed one another with the easy camaraderie of men who killed for a living. Then, with a subtle push designed to be undetectable to the cafeteria monitor, Tony sent my lunch tray clattering to the floor.

"Whoops."

"Oh, no problem," I gushed, as I leaned over to pick up the dishes. Food was smeared across the floor. "Accidents happen." I stood up. "Be right back. Gotta get some fresh dog barf!"

I rushed across the cafeteria to the food line and, when Tony turned away, slipped through the door leading to the band room.

Sophomore year was not exactly beginning with a bang.

My parents were, fortunately, clueless about this persecution. At home, I chose to suffer in silence— a sort of Gandhi with platform shoes—highlighting only the positive aspects of my school experience by showing my parents the caveat-laden praise of my junior high band director, who had written in my eighth-grade yearbook, "Stick with it, Eric. You're *finally* starting to show *signs* of *becoming* a good trumpet player." (He included the italics.)

Val, on the other hand—as a recent graduate of the school and a member of the popular set—knew the truth, and was gracious enough to discuss it with me at length.

"Well, of *course* people hate you," she said patiently as she applied extra-strength Sun-In to her hair. "I mean, you're in the marching band, for God's sake. That's right up there with understanding algebra or crying in gym class."

"Well, what do I do?" I said plaintively.

She gazed at herself thoughtfully in the mirror. "Good question. I don't exactly see you punching people out."

"'Peace cannot be achieved through violence,'"

I replied haughtily, "'it can only be achieved through understanding.' Ralph Waldo Emerson."

"Yeah, well, every now and then a good slug can do wonders." She plugged in Mother's portable suntan lamp. "But if you *have* to be a band geek—"

"Oh, I do," I assured her.

"Then maybe you should try getting into the stage band." She flipped on the sunlamp. "At least they're a little cooler. I mean, they play music from this century."

AS VAL BUSIED HERSELF frying her hair to a golden brown, I slipped down to the basement. I no longer had my Endora bedspread and, of course, as a nearly sixteen-year-old, considered the costumed conjuring I had once performed to be the silly ministrations of a child.

I was, however, becoming a bit more confident in my magical connection to God. And I now found myself in rather desperate need of his help, since the stage band—a group that played jazz and rock hits, and *was* rumored to have a measure of cool—was difficult to get into.

I closed my eyes and thought back to the day I had magically visualized myself as a member of the band Chicago. Maybe, I thought, I had aimed too high with that one. Maybe the stage band was an achievable goal.

I imagined playing a stage band concert, the trumpet section a precision group of players whose dance moves were almost as funky as their blowing. I imagined becoming first chair in that band, a standout whose star potential had been recognized by the band director, Mr. Ronson, from day one. I imagined my name on everyone's lips, mentioned in the same breath with the greats: Miles Davis, Eric Poole, the black guy from Kool and the Gang.

Whoa, I thought, pulling out of my reverie. Sorry, God. I don't mean to ask for the moon. I just want to win a place in the band, however lowly.

"Great," I felt him say silently. "Let's start with a killer audition number."

With his heavenly inspiration, I chose "Billy, Don't Be a Hero," a song with a strong melody line and a profound social message about war or something. I spent the next several weeks playing it over and over, imagining the glorious and shining moment when Mr. Ronson, the band director, would anoint me as one of the group's shiny new members.

THE DAY of the big audition, I arrived to discover numerous other members of the marching and concert bands already there. As had always been the case in band, I had developed more female friends than male—no real mystery, since girls possessed a much more satisfying sense of both humor and style.

I approached two friends, a pretty blond named Leslie Brockmeyer, who spoke in a voice so soft that you had to apply her lips directly to your ear to make out what she was saying, and Nanette Oslowski, whose dishwater-brown hair was cut short and mannish and who resembled a beagle with pierced ears.

"Your boobs are so big," I said to Nanette as she stood gossiping with Leslie, "you could keep eighteen seamen afloat in a tidal wave."

"You are such a crack-up," Leslie appeared to say as I read her lips.

"I think I just peed a little," Nanette added, which made sense given her proximity to the canine species.

I grinned. Their amusement at my wit was so intoxicating that it seemed unsportsmanlike to tell them that I had stolen the line from an Erma Bombeck book.

Suddenly we heard a voice behind us.

"Is this the foxy section?"

I turned to find Bill Pinkerton winking at Leslie. Bill was a short, good-looking senior, and what he lacked in height, he made up for in macho confidence, upper-class glamour and talent—he was first trumpet in virtually every band the school had. Had he been tall enough to see over the football, he probably would have lettered in sports instead of band.

"I suppose you and I will be first chair," he said, putting his arm around Leslie's shoulder, no mean feat since she was four inches taller. He sighed in a husky voice, flexing his pectoral muscles, which danced like marionettes under his too-tight T-shirt. "It's a heavy load to carry, but somebody's gotta shoulder the burden, right?"

Before I could ask Bill if it was easier to carry the load from a position so low to the ground, the band director called us to attention.

Mr. Ronson was a tall, slightly potbellied man with short hair that was graying at the sides. He wore Sansabelt slacks and short-sleeved dress shirts virtually every day, and was a kindhearted leader with, occasionally, the disposition of Sonny Corleone.

"The Hazelwood Central Stage Band," he said, shouting into a bullhorn although we were just standing around the band room, "is the definitive reflection of north St. Louis County's finest musical talent. Representing a group of this stature does not come without sacrifice, sweat and toil. Prepare to be worked like a Cambodian mule."

My bandmates glanced at one another, murmuring nervously. A few actually trembled. I, on the other hand, refused to be cowed by his warning. I had God on my side.

When my turn finally came to audition, I summoned all my magical courage, performing "Billy, Don't Be a Hero" with passion, with eloquence, with the inspiration, I felt, of one who was being called to greatness.

There was a long moment of silence as Mr. Ronson stared at me. Finally, he spoke. "Well, I *hate* that song. Who wants to hear about a bunch of draft dodgers?" He stood up. "You got anything else?"

I had not prepared a second number. No one had told me there'd be an encore. But I had to win him over. Without even thinking, I simply launched into the first song that came to mind, the romantic ballad "Me and Mrs. Jones," as I studied Mr. Ronson's face for any sign of approval. He just scowled.

"In the future," he announced as I concluded, "you might wanna consider a song that doesn't break one of the Ten Commandments."

"I can do 'Onward, Christian Soldiers,' if you want," I said quickly, my voice quavering a bit as I felt my one opportunity for coolness slipping from my grasp. "Or 'The Old Rugged Cross.' I do it as a jazz number."

"No, that's okay." He stuck his hand out. "Welcome to the Hazelwood Central Stage Band."

I WAS in the cool group!

I was, of course—along with Stan Copley, a shy, bookish, dark-haired fellow trumpeter—second chair to Bill Pinkerton's first chair. This wasn't a problem, since I was thrilled simply to have been accepted. Besides, Bill had been playing trumpet two years longer than Stan and I.

What *was* a problem was that it felt as though Bill possessed a civic duty to illustrate his superiority at every opportunity.

When I talked Mother and Dad into buying me a three-hundred-dollar sterling-silver trumpet, a spectacular instrument that wowed my bandmates and gave me an impressive leg up, Bill showed up with an identical one.

During breaks in rehearsal, Bill would lift his trumpet to his lips and blast an effortless high C. "Now, guys," he would say with impressive insincerity, "that's the holy grail of a trumpeter. Without that, you're nothing."

Although grateful for the magic that had helped me gain entrance into this supercool group, I began to resent the feelings of inferiority that being around Bill induced.

"I don't know why you let him get to you," Nanette said when I confided in her. "He's a troll doll with muscles. Screw him."

But Bill could hit higher notes. Bill was better-looking. Bill was a senior. I couldn't possibly screw him, I thought.

Until one rainy Wednesday afternoon, when everything changed.

THE BAND ROOM was unseasonably warm and humid this particular day, and everyone was tired, courtesy of the pep rally the marching band had had to play in the gymnasium earlier that afternoon. As we trundled through a new song, Bachman-Turner Overdrive's "Takin' Care of Business" (a hit from several years earlier, but a crowd-pleaser, according to Bill), Mr. Ronson stopped us.

"Okay, now in this part," he announced, "we're gonna try something different. I'd like to see if we can do a little jazz-rock interpretation."

Everyone stared at him questioningly.

"I want to repeat this part three times, and have a trumpet solo here," he said, indicating a specific chorus point. He pointed his baton at the trumpet section. "Bill, can you improvise sixteen bars?"

Bill looked up, a bit startled. "What?"

"Can you improvise a solo?"

"Well, ummm, sure, why not."

Bill seemed a little thrown. Sweat began to bead his brow as we began the song again from the top. I glanced over at Stan, who seemed as surprised as me. We had never seen Bill nervous. Or maybe it was just the humidity.

It all became clearer when we hit the specified part of the chorus and Bill began to play.

What issued forth from his instrument was a cacophony of musical farts that sounded less like a song and more like he was attempting to remove something stuck inside the bell of his horn.

Bill tortured it out for the requisite sixty-four beats and then abruptly stopped, to the gratitude of most everyone within earshot.

Mr. Ronson stopped us. The room was quiet.

"Uhhhhhh . . ." He glanced down. "Hmmmm." There was a long moment of silence. "Okay," he said with unconvincing cheer, as though this had been his idea all along, "Stan, your turn."

Stan next essayed the solo in heroic but uninspired fashion. Stan was a math genius who worked incredibly hard at trumpet playing, a skill that he was mastering in spite of the fact that it did not seem to come the least bit naturally to him.

"Yes," Mr. Ronson said, searching for an accolade and coming up empty. "Okay, then. Eric, you're up."

When Stan had been called upon, it had suddenly occurred to me that I would be next, and an all-encompassing panic began to rise in me. I hadn't the slightest idea what to do. And this had not been in my magical plan.

I began to shake. The room quivered like a mirage in a heat-stained desert. My breathing became shallow.

"I know this is last-minute," I mentally pleaded to God, "but I could really use your help."

As we hit the chorus, I took as deep a breath as I could muster and launched in, gamely attempting various runs and chord patterns, some of which worked, most of which didn't.

I closed my eyes. Not seeing everyone staring at me helped a bit. Then, slowly, as six bars became eight, then ten, the notes, somehow, began to come a bit easier. A bit of melody emerged. A rhythm pattern. I began to sound just like Doc Severinsen—if his bell-bottoms were too tight and someone had hit him in the head with a brick.

Within seconds, it was over. Mr. Ronson didn't stop the band at the end of the solo this time, and we played straight through to the end. When we finished, a couple of people clapped. Several others leaned forward to give me thumbs-up.

Stan punched me in the shoulder. "How did you do that?"

"Do what? It wasn't very good."

"It was better than me!"

Bill said nothing, instead busying himself by accidentally emptying his spit valve onto my suede Earth shoe.

Mr. Ronson smiled at me. "That was good, Eric," he said, a note of surprise in his voice.

I fairly floated above the band room floor. I had done something special, something unique. This was magic, squared.

But it was short-lived.

Within seconds, my moment in the sun became a dark night of the soul.

"I think we'll keep that solo in," Mr. Ronson declared. "And I have some exciting news for you all." He beamed, fairly bursting with excitement. "We're gonna play three numbers at the spring dance!"

I froze. Performing a solo in the band room was one thing. Performing it at our concert in front of classmates and parents was something else altogether. Performing it at a dance, whose attendees included seniors, the jocks, the Elites, was beyond the pale.

Bill Pinkerton put his arm around my shoulder.

"When we do the show in front of the whole school," he explained helpfully, "don't think of it as your reputation on the line. Just think of it as a learning opportunity."

I RETREATED to the basement for another talk with God.

"What have I gotten myself into?" I whispered as I sat in my old rocking chair, wistfully recalling the days when a tattered white bedspread bathed me in magic. "What if I screw it up? I'll have to quit school and become a hobo and ride the rails. And those trains are filthy."

The basement was quiet, save for the squeaking of the old rocker. Suddenly, I heard someone speak.

"What do you expect?"

I sat upright. The whole "heavenly voice" thing had been about as common an occurrence in my life as blazing shrubbery. God had always seemed to work more through inspiration than conversation. Was he actually talking to me?

"You don't believe."

There was no mistaking it this time. The voice was deep and authoritative, although it didn't quite boom the way it did in the movies. I jumped up to check the black-and-white TV in the corner. Nothing. I ran into the laundry room. "Funny, *Dad*," I hollered out, to no one. The basement was empty.

I sat back down in my chair, wondering if Val could hear this otherworldly voice upstairs. She would probably just assume it was me working on lowering my pitch again, since I was still sensitive about the recent years, when Mother couldn't tell Val and me apart on the phone and would launch into questions about my use of Kotex or whether I needed a new bra.

I glanced around, a bit embarrassed to be talking to an empty room.

"I do believe," I said, stammering. "I mean, for a while there, I wasn't so sure, but I do believe in you, I really do."

There was a long pause. And then, the voice once again.

"It's not me you need to believe in."

. . .

THE MARCH NIGHT of the spring dance was chilly, yet I stood in the band room sweating copiously in my new beige velour leisure suit, purchased especially for the occasion at Chess King. It was unclear whether my perspiration was the result of nerves or the tight polyester disco shirt I wore under it, which, although open to the fourth button, mysteriously held in body heat like a spacesuit.

The other members of the stage band seemed excited, almost giddy, obviously unaware of the potential disaster that lay ahead of us. I, meanwhile, crept down the hall to the cafeteria, to gaze through the glass window of the door.

Hundreds of students were lurching across the makeshift dance floor to the ear-shattering strains of "Love Will Keep Us Together." A few bored teachers stood around the perimeter, looking at their watches and drinking punch. I stared at the risers situated on one end of the room, the long wooden platforms that would elevate me to a moment of either triumph or disgrace. And the odds were long on triumph.

For a moment, I projected myself into my magical safe place, my cocoon, the basement. "Please," I pleaded, "show me what I need to believe in." Since that afternoon in the basement, God had been eerily, deathly silent.

Then, I heard a voice.

"Damn. Lotta people out there." Bill Pinkerton was standing beside me on tiptoe, attempting to peer out the window. "I'd hate to be you right about now."

"I'll be fine," I said unconvincingly.

"Sure you will. It'll be fun," he said brightly. "Look at it this way. It's not like people think you're cool now, right? I mean, what do you have to lose?"

Having heard this, Nanette Oslowski sidled up next to Bill. "Don't you have cookies to make in a tree somewhere?"

I smiled gratefully at her as Bill marched off, losing himself in a sea of five-foot-nine giants as the rest of the band gathered at the door.

She saw my tense expression. "You'll be great," she said matter-of-factly, and reached out to tap my chest. "You've got everything you need right in here."

Before I could respond, Mr. Ronson called us to attention.

"Okay," he said brightly, "let's have some *fun* out there!"

One by one we filed out, virtually invisible to the couples who busily groped each other to the tune of Minnie Riperton's "Lovin' You." As we stepped onto the risers, however, our platform shoes clomping loudly across the groaning wooden planks, the crowd looked up, annoyed, their intimate moment shattered.

Stan and I took our places in front of Bill, who

had asked to be on the riser above us—since, as I had explained to Stan, standing next to tall guys made it appear as though he had lost Snow White and the other dwarves.

As we stood in place, awaiting the end of the song, I gazed out at the several hundred attendees crammed into the cafeteria. I caught the eye of Theresa Weingarten, a blond goddess, who rolled her eyes at us and whispered something to her date. He laughed.

As Minnie concluded her dog-pitch destruction of the tweeters, Mr. Ronson made a signal to the deejay, who accidentally yanked the turntable needle across the 45, ruining what little of the romantic mood that remained. The crowd hissed.

"Hello!" Mr. Ronson hollered into the microphone.

He paused for applause. Everyone just stood there.

"As you know, I'm Mr. Ronson, the band director . . ."

Several people booed. He glanced around the room, scowling.

"And I'm proud to present . . ." He leaned too close into the microphone, which responded by shrieking an approximately 300-decibel feedback whine.

"Jesus!" somebody yelled. "What are you, retarded?"

"Who said that?" Mr. Ronson yelled into the microphone, scanning the crowd for the culprit. "Who said that?!"

This was not an auspicious start.

The principal hurried up to the stage to calm Mr. Ronson. They conferred for a moment, and finally, Mr. Ronson stepped back up to the mike, a forced smile pasted across his face.

"And I'm proud to present to you a special performance by Hazelwood Central's very own Stage Band!"

We launched into our first number, "Boogie Fever."

Nothing happened.

We played, loudly and enthusiastically, the band sounding tight and surprisingly good. But the crowd just stood around, staring blankly at us, a few people trying to talk above the din. The song felt as though it were taking hours.

Sweat began to pour from me as if a spigot had been installed in my forehead. Holy crap, I thought, if they're this hostile now, imagine how they'll be if I screw up my solo. Any hope I had once held of the stage band being my entrée to some measure of acceptance was evaporating right before my eyes.

Suddenly, in the corner of the cafeteria, I noticed a small clump of people beginning to dance.

Then, another.

And another.

And then, within about a minute, most of the crowd was gyrating.

We finished the song to a smattering of applause

and a few smiles, although the fact that no one was hurling fruit was enough for me.

Our second number was "Best of My Love," the Eagles ballad that gave guys all across the cafeteria an opportunity to get to second base while standing up. Couples swayed around the floor, everyone now seeming to tolerate, if not almost enjoy, the music. Another smattering of applause greeted us as we finished, this one even a bit bigger than the first.

But the real test was yet to come. Our final number was "Takin' Care of Business," and as the drummer Ryan prepared to pound out the four-beat count-off on his sticks, I thought about what God, and Nanette, had said to me.

From the first note, the crowd seemed to be really enjoying this one. Everyone began doing the Bump, and I could see freshmen and seniors alike mouthing the words as we played. Their delight almost made matters worse. The pressure was now on me not to ruin it. I held the finale of the stage band's performance, the gratification of the crowd and my own fate in my hands.

And suddenly, in a moment worthy of Miss Marple, I understood.

One, two, three, four.

Mr. Ronson raised his hand.

Five, six, seven, eight.

I took a shallow breath and began to blow.

The first few notes were, to everyone's dismay, soft and uncommanding. No one was even looking at me.

"Louder!" Stan shouted into my good ear.

Believe.

I blew harder.

The sound was still weak, the melody uninspired. A few people turned to watch me, which only made things worse.

I closed my eyes.

Believe.

As three bars became four, and four became five, something within me, slowly but surely, began to take control. And as five bars became six, then seven, then eight, I found myself creating melodies. Real, actual melodies.

Believe.

I paused to take a quick breath, and to my utter shock, the crowd, thinking I was finished, began to politely applaud.

I kept going, and, emboldened, I pulled out all the stops. When I hit the sixteenth bar on a high D, a note I wasn't even sure I could reach, a much bigger ovation began to build. What felt like a roar of approval swept over the band, and me, as the crowd danced along.

When we finished, Mr. Ronson grabbed the mike.

"And on trumpet, Mr. Eric Poole!"

The crowd in the Hazelwood Central cafeteria, most of whom didn't know—or had never cared about—the tall, skinny nerd taking a bow, whooped their approval.

As I glanced around the room, a lump in my throat so huge I could barely swallow, I noticed two middle-aged people standing in the back of the room. They weren't teachers. They weren't administrators. They were my parents.

Dad was smiling bigger than I had ever seen him smile. Mother had tears in her eyes. Dad put his fingers in his mouth to whistle as a teacher leaned over to say something to them, and Mother pointed at me and nodded, her face beaming.

I smiled back at them, wanting to capture everything about this moment: Dad's brown corduroy sport jacket, Mother's dusty rose skirt. I wanted to memorize their expressions and the glow that seemed to emanate from them. I had always known that they loved me, but I had never known that they were proud.

They gave a small wave and slipped out the door. Parents weren't supposed to be at the dance.

As we swept out of the cafeteria and back down the hall to the band room, various band members patted me on the back.

"Wow—you were great!"

"You really rocked!"

"That was amazing!"

In those short seconds of attention and affection and appreciation, as I stood basking in the approval of my bandmates, I knew that something had changed. That not only had I earned some small measure of acceptance by the school at large, but that the creation of that moment had come from within.

As we entered the band room, Bill passed by, taking pains to ignore the commotion surrounding me. Nanette turned to him.

"Guess you got a little competition for first chair, huh?"

Bill rolled his eyes and snorted.

"Course," Nanette said, turning back to me, "you'll have to remove the booster seat."

I STOOD in the garage, the glow of my stage band triumph the week before still fresh in my mind as I scavenged through boxes for tchotchkes with which to redecorate my room.

Now that I was gaining a measure of popularity, it stood to reason that I might, at some point, actually have people over, and my current decor smacked of tragic early teendom.

I paused to watch Dad as he hung a tennis ball on a string from the ceiling. The ball stopped about five feet above the ground.

"That seems a little high for a cat," I said, surveying his work. "Plus, we don't have a cat."

"It's for your mother," Dad said, whispering, since the door to the backyard was open.

For the last few years, Mother had been attempting to turn herself into a Nubian goddess by spending every daylight hour that she wasn't cleaning stretched out on the patio in a ten-year-old bikini held together by safety pins and duct tape. This wasn't as problematic in the warmer months, but it did pose its challenges when the temperature was forty-eight degrees, a trial she overcame by simply pulling a sheet up to her neck.

"I didn't even know she liked tennis."

"She doesn't. It's to help her pull the car in."

Of Mother's many extraordinary talents, driving was not one of them. She tended to treat the piloting of an automobile as though it was a Six Flags bumper car, bashing into the side of the garage with such regularity that we had stopped fixing the car. The tennis ball was a bid to keep her from demolishing Dad's workbench.

It wasn't that she lacked depth perception; she simply felt that cautious driving consumed precious time that could be devoted to more important pursuits, like polishing all the lacquer off the furniture.

I rifled through a box. "Oh, my *Mad* magazines!" I said, delighted. "I wondered where these went."

"Giveaway!" Mother hollered from the patio.

"Hey," I yelled back, "maybe I still want these!"

"You're almost sixteen. Do you want your old *Highlights* magazines, too?"

She had a point. I had moved on to more intellectual publications, like *Parade* and *People*.

With a wistful sigh, I wrote "Disabled Veterans" on the box, the name of our charity of choice since (a) Dad was a Korean War vet, and (b) they picked up from your front porch. I imagined the joy and uplift these magazines would bring to men who had no legs, and was, for a moment, consumed with admiration at my generosity of spirit.

"You're gonna have to go faster than that or we're gonna be here all day," Dad said, "and your mother wants me to wax the garage floor."

I moved on to another box. It was costume jewelry of Mother's.

"Do you want this old jewelry?" I yelled to Mother.

"Disabled Veterans!" she hollered back. Good choice, I thought, since these vets probably had sons like me who might wish to, at some point as an innocent young child, don their mother's pantsuits and bangle bracelets in an unconscious ode to Florence Henderson.

As I flipped one flap of the box closed, something lying beneath the jewelry caught my eye. I pushed aside the necklaces and chokers, the earrings and bracelets, being careful to avoid getting stabbed by a stray brooch. What lay beneath was white. It had stringy fringe. It was dusty.

It was my old bedspread.

I gasped involuntarily as I pulled it out of the box, the jewelry clanking and tinkling as pieces fell one over the other.

"What?" Dad said as he measured the distance from the tennis ball to the floor.

"Nothing," I replied. "I just thought Mother had given this away."

He spotted the bedspread. "She was going to," he said, "but then she told me to put it in a box."

As I thumbed the threadbare fabric, I saw the faith that I had imbued into this simple old piece of cloth, determined to prove that with its help, each new day would be better, and kinder, and more hopeful than the last.

But I was, I realized, beginning to discover a new kind of magic, one that came from within. I still believed that God and I were a team, but the magic had to begin with me.

I carefully folded up the mound of fabric, realizing that this would truly be the last time I touched it. I hope it goes to some other eight-year-old who's scared, I thought. I hope it gives him the comfort it gave me.

As I tucked the bedspread back into the box, patting it carefully into place, the smell of coconut tanning oil flooded my senses. I looked up to find Mother standing next to me, holding her ragged bikini top in place.

"Well, would you look at that," she said, whispering so that Dad wouldn't hear. "Endora lives again."